Slander constitutes a central social, legal and literary concern of early modern England. A category of discourse which transgresses the law, it offers a more historically grounded and fluid account of power relations between poets and the state than that offered by the commonly accepted model of official censorship. An investigation of slander reveals it to be an effective, unstable and reversible means of repudiating one's opposition that could be deployed by rulers or poets. Spenser, Jonson and Shakespeare each use the paradigm of slander to challenge official criticism of poetry, while contemporary legal theory associates slander with poetry. However, even as rulers themselves make use of slander in the form of propaganda to demonize those they perceive to be their foes, ultimately they are unable to contain completely the threat posed by slanderous accusations against the state.

Cambridge Studies in Renaissance Literature and Culture 19

The culture of slander in early modern England

Since the 1970s there has been a broad and vital reinterpretation of the nature of literary texts, a move away from formalism to a sense of literature as an aspect of social, economic, political, and cultural history. While the earliest New Historicist work was criticized for a narrow and anecdotal view of history, it also served as an important stimulus for poststructuralist, feminist, Marxist, and psychoanalytical work, which in turn has increasingly informed and redirected it. Recent writing on the nature of representation, the historical construction of gender and of the concept of identity itself, on theatre as a political and economic phenomenon and on the ideologies of art generally, reveals the breadth of the field. Cambridge Studies in Renaissance Literature and Culture is designed to offer historically oriented studies of Renaissance literature and theatre which make use of the insights afforded by theoretical perspectives. The view of history envisioned is above all a view of our own history, a reading of the Renaissance for and from our own time.

Recent titles include

Knowledge, discovery, and imagination in early modern Europe: the rise of aesthetic rationalism
TIMOTHY J. REISS, New York University

The project of prose in early modern Europe and the New World
edited by ELIZABETH FOWLER, Yale University, and
ROLAND GREENE, University of Oregon

The marketplace of print: pamphlets and the public sphere in early modern England
ALEXANDRA HALASZ, Dartmouth College

Courtly letters in the age of Henry VIII: literary culture and the arts of deceit
SETH LERER, Stanford University

A complete list of books in the series is given at the end of the volume

The culture of slander in early modern England

M. Lindsay Kaplan
Georgetown University

CAMBRIDGE
UNIVERSITY PRESS

CAMBRIDGE UNIVERSITY PRESS
Cambridge, New York, Melbourne, Madrid, Cape Town, Singapore, São Paulo

Cambridge University Press
The Edinburgh Building, Cambridge CB2 2RU, UK

Published in the United States of America by Cambridge University Press, New York

www.cambridge.org
Information on this title: www.cambridge.org/9780521584081

First published 1997
This digitally printed first paperback version 2006

A catalogue record for this publication is available from the British Library

Library of Congress Cataloguing in Publication data

Lindsay, Kaplan M.
The culture of slander in early modern England / M. Lindsay Kaplan.
p. cm. – (Cambridge studies in Renaissance literature and culture : 19)
Includes bibliographical references and index.
ISBN 0 52158408 6 (hardback).
1. English literature – Early modern, 1500–1700 – History and criticism.
2. Libel and slander – England – History – 16th century.
3. Libel and slander – England – History – 17th century.
4. Literature and society – England – History.
5. Libel and slander in literature. 6. Renaissance – England.
7. Law and literature. I. Title. II. Series.
PR428.L53156 1997
820.9′355–dc21 96–45539 CIP

ISBN-13 978-0-521-58408-1 hardback
ISBN-10 0-521-58408-6 hardback

ISBN-13 978-0-521-58637-5 paperback
ISBN-10 0-521-58637-2 paperback

This book is dedicated to my family, Anne, Jerry and Rachel, and to the memory of Perino Boone Wingfield.

And let the beauty of the Lord our God be upon us:
and establish thou the work of our hands upon us;
yea, the work of our hands establish thou it.

Psalm 90:17, *King James Bible*

Contents

Acknowledgments

I am deeply grateful to the many teachers, colleagues, friends and family members who contributed to this project, which in some sense originated in my first year of college. I was fortunate enough to begin my education in early modern English literature at Johns Hopkins University, where I studied with, among others, Leo Braudy, Stanley Fish, Arnold Stein, Barry Weller and Stephen Orgel, my affectionately idiosyncratic friend and mentor for half my lifetime. I am deeply indebted to him for his consistent interest in my work and for his encouragement in revising and completing this book. Stephen's guidance led me to Berkeley for graduate school and to Stephen Greenblatt as my advisor, without whom I could not have written this project. Thanks are owed as well to my other dissertation readers, Paul Alpers and Robert Post, as well as to the University of California English Department for providing teaching and fellowship support. I also appreciate the encouragement and stimulus I received from other friends and teachers while at Berkeley and afterwards: Alpers' Dissertation group, Oliver Arnold, Harry Berger, Jr., Richard Burt, Natalie Charkow and John Hollander, Jennifer Clarvoe, Fran Dolan, Frances Ferguson, Louis Galdieri, Cathy Gallagher, David Gewanter, Cynthia Giddle, Inderpal Grewal, Mark Maslan, Walter Benn Michaels, Anne Middleton, Rhonda Rockwell, Eve Sanders, James Shapiro, Valerie Traub and Kerry Walk. Special thanks go to Katherine Eggert who was and remains an insightful, energetic and generous reader of much I have written. For my researches in England I am especially indebted to the staff of Lincoln's Inn Library, and to R. H. Helmholz, who provided invaluable assistance at the early stages of my project. The revision of the dissertation was significantly aided during my first years of teaching at Lewis and Clark College by my students, my colleagues in the English Department, especially

Annie Dawid, the Feminist Reading Group, and the receipt of summer research grants as well as a junior sabbatical. The Folger Shakespeare Library also provided important assistance in the form of a Short-Term Fellowship and as an invaluable resource of texts and colleagues since then. I am grateful to Northwestern University Press for allowing me permission to reprint "Slander for Slander in *Measure for Measure*," which first appeared in an earlier version in *Renaissance Drama* ns xxi, *Disorder and the Drama*, edited by Mary Beth Rose and published by Northwestern University Press and the Newberry Library Center for Renaissance Studies. Copyright © 1991 by Northwestern University Press. All rights reserved; reprinted by permission of Northwestern University Press. I am appreciative of audiences at various conferences where I have been able to present earlier versions of this work: the New Languages for the Stage Conference at the University of Kansas, Spenser at Kalamazoo (with special thanks to Jerry Dees), the Renaissance Society of America, and the Folger Institute Evening Colloquium. My most recent debts include those to my friends and associates at Georgetown University who have provided a warm and encouraging environment in which to complete this project, especially Leona Fisher, Kim Hall, Patricia O'Connor, Michael Ragussis, Amy Robinson, Jason Rosenblatt, Jim Slevin, Bruce Smith and Kathy Temple. A reduced course load and a Summer Faculty Research Grant also greatly expedited the book's final stages here at Georgetown. Finally, and dearest, are the members of my family, some of whom did not live to see the completion of this project, all of whom have loved me and encouraged me along the way. Love and thanks to Susan and Harvey Kayman, Ben and Ruth Goluboff, Margaret Lindsay Wingfield, Marian Bergman, Arnold and Caroline Roth, and to the dedicatees of this book: my mother, father and sister and to the memory of my beloved grandfather whose agile and open mind offered a model of thoughtful exploration for thirty-five years of my life.

Introduction: censorship versus slander

This book advances the argument that slander provides a model crucial for the analysis of power relations between poets and state[1] in early modern England, and by extension that the concept of censorship, currently employed by critics of early modern English literature to discuss these relations, serves rather to limit and distort our understanding. In recent years, critical interest in power in the early modern period has taken up the question of the nature and extent of control the state was able to exercise over literary expression, as well as explored the capacity for resistance or challenge that literature could pose to political authority. These discussions have for the most part assumed or explicitly articulated a paradigm of censorship as the appropriate context for analyzing power relations between the poet and the state. However, the use of censorship, particularly of the drama, as an analytic focus poses a few problems. The term is often employed anachronistically in presupposing a hierarchical exercise of power only possible for a centralized state bureaucracy and thus inapplicable to early modern England. Typically, the narrow focus on regulatory mechanisms and topical content employed by scholars of censorship prevents our understanding how the control of literary production was shaped by, and shaped, larger socio-political concern in the period over the control of language in general. While discussions of censorship in the past decade made some valuable contributions to our understanding of early modern English texts, they virtually ignored the significance of defamation, a critical concern that fueled official attempts in England to control a whole range of discourses from the Reformation forward. That defamation posed a serious problem for the individual at all levels of early modern society suggests that we need to situate our examination of state control of poetry within this larger context of language that transgresses the law.

The dramatic rise in defamation in sixteenth-century England seems to take the common law establishment by surprise, judging from the inconsistent and sometimes contradictory redresses that develop in response to the phenomenon.[2] In addition to the definitional problems the law had in responding to slander, there are also linguistic and material obstacles to the effective control of transgressive language. It is impossible to control what people say and how this will be interpreted. The regular and wide-ranging circulation of libels, ballads, epigrams and other forms of defamatory speech or writing in early modern England testifies to the state's impotence in the suppression of criticism. Further, the state's own employment of a range of defamatory practices to control, humiliate or demonize its populace and its enemies implicates it in the very transgressions it ostensibly seeks to silence. By taking defamation as our model, we are able to see the places in which the state was not able to control transgressive language rather than focusing on those moments, as the censorship model does, where it was. While defining a legitimate means of official response to transgressive language, censorship is nevertheless a subcategory of the laws and responses to defamation; as a focus, it assumes a very restricted legal, social and political role for literature. When we understand, as contemporaries did, censorship and literature itself in their larger cultural contexts, we can see their participation in the processes of defamatory discourse. In so doing, we can substitute the repressive model censorship offers with a more complex and contestatory account of the operation of power with regards to language which accords a measure of agency and resistance less available in analyses of censorship.

An examination of the limitations of the censorship model is necessary before we can understand the centrality of defamation for power relations between poets and the state. Annabel Patterson's influential *Censorship and Interpretation* advances an argument for reading relations between rulers and poets within a historical–political framework. However, the lens through which Patterson chooses to view her subject distorts her analysis; while acknowledging that language poses real political problems in sixteenth- and seventeenth-century England, she dilutes the historical specificity of her claims in presenting a transhistorical notion of censorship:

I hope to show where this study might fit into a much larger investigation, not only of censorship throughout Europe in the early modern period, but also of the cultural impact of censorship since then, in Eastern Europe, for example, or Latin America. In addition, my central thesis, that it is to censorship that we in part owe our very concept of "literature," as a kind of discourse with rules of its own, is obviously capable, if true, of great extension; not least because its acceptance might require a review of that other set of unexamined assumptions, about the freedom of the literary, or the critical, or the textual from historical concerns. (Patterson 1984: 3–4)

This claim suggests that all authors in all periods in all countries respond to all political control of writing in a similar manner. While this move insists on the political nature of poetry formation, and rightly calls for an exploration of how society understands and shapes the literary, it undermines rather than establishes a connection between poetry and "historical concerns." Poetry indeed intersects with the political, but this relationship is in flux; while something may be gained by sketching out transhistorical patterns in the poetical–political relationship, its social significance can be better understood by attempting to discern the dynamic as it manifests itself at discrete historical moments.

Patterson's account of censorship not only assumes that its operation is the same across time but also that it does not require definition. Her real interests lie in the hermeneutics, not the mechanisms, of censorship; by concentrating on what are essentially its literary aspects she replicates the theoretical position her book argues against by ignoring the social and material aspects of the problem.

My own approach to censorship focuses only occasionally on law and the formal institutions and mechanisms whereby the press, or the pulpit, or the theatrical companies were theoretically made subject to state control. The legal history of censorship in relationship to all aspects of the printing trade has been well covered by F. S. Siebert, among others. (Patterson 1984: 10)

While Siebert acknowledges some connection between the regulation of the press and libel law, his narrow handling of the subject distorts legal history and offers an absurdly totalitarian view of Stuart censorship.[3] More problematic for Patterson, though, is the suggestion that an examination of censorship does not need to consider seriously the material, legal and social aspects of the process. While she does acknowledge that "there were certain moments in [the history of censorship] when the law was forced to take particular cognizance of problems of interpretation" (Patterson 1984: 10) she intimates that this process is episodic. This assumption prevents her from viewing the issue as part of a continuum in which the control of texts at any given point in history is situated in relation to larger social anxieties about the control of language.

While Patterson's definition of censorship remains implicit, she is quite explicit in her discussion of its effects on interpretation. She sees the production of literary texts in early modern society as "essentially a joint project, a cultural bargain between writers and political leaders":

> It is a central part of my project to show how the historical condition of an era of censorship united writers and readers in a common interest as to how interpretation in fact worked, how it could be carried out in any given sociopolitical situation, how the interaction between writers and readers could be formulated in ways that were intelligible (in law) and useful (in politics). (Patterson 1984: 7)

According to Patterson, the uncertainty of language created a safety-valve of ambiguity which both sides were usually happy with.

> For what we find everywhere apparent and widely understood, from the middle of the sixteenth century in England, is a system of communication in which ambiguity becomes a creative and necessary instrument, a social and cultural force of considerable consequence. (Patterson 1984: 10–11)

While this "joint project" might be imagined as a means of criticizing policies of the state, the argument's logic suggests that the potential for challenging the status quo is limited, since poets must, in effect, obtain official approval for their words. In spite of what I take to be Patterson's interest in showing the liberty that ambiguity allowed to authors, the structure of her model suggests that the state defines what can be written or spoken and the poet, more or less, acquiesces.[4]

Unlike Patterson's *Censorship and Interpretation*, which fully develops a theory of the hermeneutics that evolves out of censorship while ignoring the mechanisms of that control, Janet Clare's *Art Made Tongue-tied by Authority* attends explicitly to the process of dramatic censorship and rigorously documents specific cases of official alteration of or intervention in the text or performance of plays. However, in spite of the book's meticulous scholarship, attempts to reconstruct and analyze the logic of the censoring process remain speculative because in many cases the evidence, the material cut from a play, is lost. In further contrast to Patterson, Clare's conclusion denies even the measure of theoretical autonomy and self-consciousness that the former accords early modern writers:

> It is frequently acknowledged that censorship gives birth to metaphors which thrive on ambiguity . . . Arguably, such ambiguity can enrich a play and censorship can actually mould style and composition to positive effect. Yet in its incursions against freedom of expression and in its distortion of the text, censorship has pernicious results . . . all the plays of our period were written in the shadow of the censor and . . . no dramatist could unchain his thoughts from the agent of that most arbitrary and punitive instrument of state control. (Clare 1990: 214–15)

Clare assumes an all-powerful mechanism of state censorship which succeeds not only in controlling the written products of dramatists, but also their unspoken thoughts.

In *Mastering the Revels*, Richard Dutton makes a valuable contribution to the representations of power relations between poet and the state as sketched out in the two earlier works. He demonstrates convincingly that the conflicting factions at court obviated the application of any consistent principle of censorship to or control of dramatic texts. However, his conclusions are surprisingly reminiscent of Patterson:

> The basic contention of this book is that the whole system of a factional court, supported by a complex inter-weaving of patronage, conspired in most circumstances to "allow" a wide range of comment on contemporary affairs, so long as this was properly licensed, suitably veiled and not slanted with offensive particularity at a powerful constituency. (Dutton 1991: 178)

Here too poetic resistance seems to be precluded by the assumption of compliance with the, albeit fragmented, will of the court. While Dutton convincingly demonstrates the permeability and instability of monarchic and aristocratic power, he nevertheless uses censorship, defined as a "form of repression" (Dutton 1991: ix), as the context for his discussion of poet–state relations.

Although Richard Burt's *Licensed by Authority* extends the excellent insights of Dutton's work in demonstrating the fluidity of power relations between poets and censors, he breaks sharply with all previous accounts of censorship which anachronistically situate the censoring function solely within the state. According to his argument,

> Censorship . . . pervaded early Stuart theatrical culture: it was practiced and nurtured not only by the court but also by playwrights, theatrical entrepreneurs, printers, poets, courtiers, and critics. Thus, the broad questions critics have regularly asked about the theater – Who was for or against censorship? Was this text oppositional or orthodox? – simply do not make sense. Though some dramatists defended "liberty of speech," that liberty always entailed some form of censorship. Dramatists and patrons did not group themselves in opposition to censorship, or in favor of it. Rather, they debated who should censor and who have liberty, for what ends and on what grounds, and their struggle was registered in a contest over the meanings of the words *liberty* and *censorship* themselves. (Burt 1993: x–xi)

Burt argues that the early modern concept of censorship was not understood as the exclusive right of the state, and that the poet-critic, as epitomized by Ben Jonson, while subject to censorship, could also perform the censor's critical function, or even be in line to serve as Master of the Revels himself.

In spite of the different foci organizing these analyses of censorship, they all share a blind spot. Implicit in each of these works is the understanding that censorship is connected in some way to defamation, but the structure, process and significance of infamy remain unexplored.[5] Patterson sees William Prynne's 1633 trial for seditious libel as a "paradigmatic case . . . and extraordinarily relevant to the questions this book poses, about how the state functioned as a 'reader' of texts, about the role and status of ambiguity in the reading process" (Patterson 1984: 10). However, Prynne's case is also atypical, in Patterson's view, in that in coming to trial it represents "an exceptional failure, a dramatic breakdown of the normal methods of dealing with those problems" (Patterson 1984: 10). In assuming that the legal concerns raised by transgressive discourse are only expressed exceptionally in prosecution, Patterson fails to consider the body of law developed around defamation and its significance for shaping larger cultural expectations about what can and cannot be said or written. While Clare attempts to present a contemporary definition of libel, "the concept of public libel carried the thrust of sedition and destabilisation as well as slander," she incorrectly suggests that the legal scope of defamation is articulated by royal proclamation (Clare 1990: 61). Although she asserts that "this dual aspect of libel . . . became the focus of censorship, dramatic and non-dramatic," so that, in effect, defamation is the primary force shaping official regulation of texts, she fails to consider the ecclesiastical, statute, criminal, and common law definitions of and redresses for defamation (Clare 1990: 61). Without a fuller account of libel and slander, it is impossible to understand their significance for the process of censorship.

Dutton, on the other hand, does not explicitly acknowledge that censorship is tied to the structure of defamation. However, in the course of his analysis he does repeatedly reveal connections between the two. In a telling example, he cites a 1551 proclamation as "the first definite attempt to institute a formal system of licensing of materials to be performed, which implicitly also meant censorship" (Dutton 1991: 19). Its targeted audience includes "'vagabondes, tellers of newes, sowers of sedicious rumours, players, and printers without licence, and divers other disordred persons' . . . forbidding, on pain of fine and imprisonment, the printing, sale or distribution of anything written in English, without the express permission of the king or the Privy Council" (Dutton 1991: 19). He situates the foundation of censorship within the context of an act concerned with the control of a range of transgressive and unlawful discourse often associated with defamation. For the most part, however, Dutton ignores the contemporary language and thus structure for dealing with the problem of disruptive language, and therefore fails to see how official attempts to identify and marginalize oppositional discourse in dramatic texts connect with larger concerns about infamy.

Burt makes frequent reference to defamation in *Licensed by Authority* and even sketches out its relation to censorship.

> I propose . . . that we think of censorship broadly as a mechanism for legitimating and delegitimating access to discourse. Censorship in its usual sense – the repression of sedition, libel, or blasphemy – was only one mechanism for regulating the circulation of discourses, exchanges of power between institutions, transfers of status markers from one institution to another, and so on which marked the emergence of a licensed and relatively autonomous aesthetic domain. To define literary censorship as an activity that legitimates and delegitimates discourses and their modes of circulation means broadening the term, so that its negative, repressive function is seen as only one of many regulatory mechanisms. (Burt 1993: 12–13)

However, he never explains or explores the contemporary meaning of "libel," a term undergoing significant redefinition in the period with which he is concerned. Without a fuller account of defamation and how it might be influenced by or even influence the process of censorship, the significance of this relationship is largely occluded. While I agree that it is crucial to think of the control of literary production in terms of legitimating and delegitimating access to discourse, I would differ with Burt's identification of censorship as the primary mechanism for this process. In his account, concerns about libel represent a sub-category within the domain of censorship. What I would like to argue is that the discourses of censorship Burt examines develop out of larger social concerns regarding transgressive language, usually understood as defamation.

Before turning to a fuller account of slander, I would like to suggest some of the inadequacies of censorship as a model for understanding power relations between the poet and the state. Even if one imagines censorship, as Burt does, in terms of an activity that can be performed by poet-critics as well as official censors, the process nevertheless constitutes a "regulatory mechanism" which confers a measure of authority on the censor. Literary criticism, "as a form of regulation . . . was already paradoxically implicated in censorship. Criticism authorized censors to repress or to exercise discursive liberties. Moreover, the critic and the censor were complicit rather than opposed: censors operated as critics, and critics legitimated particular kinds of censorship, demanding that authors submit to critical censure" (Burt 1993: 30). Burt demonstrates Jonson's capacity to appropriate the structure of official censorship in the poet's ability to censure or criticize inferior or unsuitable texts; however, this effectually validates the state's means of control. Although, as Burt argues, Jonson makes distinctions between legitimate and illegitimate censorship (Burt 1993: 28), the model does not really allow a means for contesting the state's capacity to alter or suppress texts or speech. Delegitimizing censorship is here effected by replacing it with another, legitimate criticism. However, the paradigm remains one that only registers repression, hence reproducing and authorizing state control. The critic's censoring function is analogous to, but not reciprocal with, the state's. Both poet-critic and state-censor have the authority to alter texts or speech; but while the censorship model provides the state with a means of controlling poetry, it does not allocate to poets an equivalent means with which they can control, or, more accurately, resist regulation.

Burt ultimately claims that censorship is inescapable, using the metaphor of neurosis to suggest a range of censoring functions (revision, criticism, censorship); "there is a permanent difficulty in recognizing the difference between the 'real' text and its later distortions precisely because there is no original, precensored text to be (dis)-covered" (Burt 1993: 51). While this may be the case, it is not the only way of understanding how a text works. By focusing on what is *done to* the text, we lose sight of what a text can do. While Burt claims that criticism can function transgressively (Burt 1993: 51–2), the overwhelming force of his argument serves to present the text as passively acted upon, rather than itself functioning as an agent.

Censorship offers a model of repression; to say there is no escape from censorship is to suggest that repression always succeeds. Even if you argue, as Burt does, that censorship serves to legitimate as well as delegitimate discourse (Burt 1993: 13), you assume the legitimate authority of the censor. Slander shifts the structure of the paradigm to offer a *response* to censorship which challenges the authority of censors by redefining their criticisms as misunderstandings, or more aggressively, defamations – they make a libel where the poet made a play. Hence, it provides a model of power that is reversible rather than hierarchical. This account understands power as more evenly distributed between poet and state, revealing that their relation is much more contestatory, and the playing field in the struggle to define legitimate language is closer to level. Slander can put you on the offensive; rather than defensively anticipating and perhaps incorporating your opponent's criticism into your thinking and writing, an accusation of slander enables you to delegitimate an opposing epistemological paradigm. You might not succeed in making your charge stick, but you nevertheless possess grounds to challenge your repressor. Slander offers a model of contestation, rather than repression and regulation, which demonstrates the material consequences linguistic instability has for the social order.

In its most general sense, slander is a false accusation which results in the humiliation of its victims. Slander law attempts to control this language, which is seen to pose various threats to the social order. However, the slander paradigm does not merely replace the censorship model of controlling transgressive language with a more wide-ranging mechanism of repression. For what we discover when we look at slander and slander law is the incredible instability of the categories of legitimate and illegitimate speech. Not only are charges of slander reversible, but the very structure of slander law, as I will argue in the next chapter, is itself riven with inconsistencies.

An example of the difficulties of negotiating the complexities of slander counter-accusations can be found in a Star Chamber case of 1604. A suit was brought by one Harris claiming that he had been harassed and defamed by Newcomin, a fellow preacher who wrote a libel against him and the state of the Church of England. The libel, reproduced in the Star Chamber bill, takes the form of a poem protesting popishness. With regard to this failing in the laity, Newcomin exhibits a certain charitableness: "therefore exhorte them patientlie theire error for to see / and in love, pittie and comforte theire poore distressed estate / for sclanderous raylinge is the way to make them further of[f] then nowe" (PRO, STAC 8 177/05). Patient persuasion motivated by love will convert the straying, while berating them will further alienate them. What is interesting here is that while the speaker rejects slanderous attacks, he seems to do so on pragmatic, not legal or moral, grounds. This is not a surprising attitude given that the speaker has been charged with slander. In attacking Harris, a member of the ecclesiastical hierarchy, with a defamatory poem, Newcomin would appear to endorse slander of Anglican clerics:

> You shall finde [the laity] certainely neerer god then a covetous prelate exacting mightilie,
> Uppon honest men cruellie as hath been manifestlie seene
>
> . . .
>
> But when he lookes to please the Devill and himself by raylinge,
> Then shall you hear him stronglie sounding speeches shrille and odde
>
> . . .
>
> Nor christian man of faithe and knowledge founde that ever I did heare
> But thought him like Kayne or Saul for malice, like Haman for pride
> Like Balaam for covetousnes, like Ahitophell for counsell it is cleere
> And like Naballe for churlyshenes, yea he hath a slanderous tonge be side.

Strikingly, though, Newcomin paradoxically defames his victim by accusing him of railing and slander. Relying on scriptural evidence for support, he literally demonizes his opponent to justify his position. The slipperiness of slander, both in identifying and prosecuting it, shows the real difficulty in policing transgressive speech on all social levels in early modern England.

Defamation does not only offer a more complex model of power, it also represents the context in which censorship developed in early modern England. By focusing on censorship, scholars have failed to understand the larger challenges facing official attempts to control discourse. An analysis of defamation takes the larger social problem of transgressive language – slander marks a place where words come in conflict with the law – and provides a framework within which some of the problems that poetry posed for society can be articulated. But I am not merely asserting that, since concerns about slander shaped censorship, there is necessarily a relation between slander and poetry. On the contrary, both contemporary poets and legal theorists articulate this connection, although often from opposing perspectives. Poetry and drama are regularly associated with slander in official definitions of transgressive discourse; conversely, poets frequently deny charges that their work constitutes defamation, and counter that such accusations are themselves defamatory. Furthermore, as evidenced in the above court case, a review of libels from the period reveals that poetry was considered an excellent medium for defamation by its malicious practitioners. Let us now turn to an analysis of the development and significance of the structures of slander in early modern English culture in order to understand their consequences for literature and literary representations of power relations between the state and the poet.[6]

1 The paradox of slander

To gain a sense of the scope and operation of early modern defamation, one might begin with the complexity and contradiction contained in the definition of the various terms used to denote it. I should explain at this point that I tend to privilege the use of "slander" as a general term, following general usage of common parlance and the central courts in the late sixteenth and early seventeenth centuries, which employ various expressions for false imputations interchangeably. Because distinctions in the terms "libel" and "slander" were still unclear during this period, legal historians tend to use the term "defamation" to cover both safely. Although the Star Chamber tended to see written defamation as a more serious offense than spoken defamation, the common law courts did not consistently distinguish them as libel and slander respectively until 1660 (Baker 1990: 506). This ambiguity of terms is evident in the language of bills presented to the Star Chamber alleging defamatory attacks in poetry and drama, in legal treatises on the subject and even in state proclamations and statutes; take, for example, this 1581 statute making it a felony to "deuise, and write, print, or set foorth, anie maner of booke, rime, ballad, letter or writing conteining any false, seditious, and slanderous matter to the defamation of the queenes majestie" (23 Eliz.c.2). As F. G. Emmison notes: "Libel and slander, for our purposes, scarcely need to be distinguished, for the scandalous writing, if in ballad form, was also meant to be sung" (Emmison 1970: 66).[1]

While slander is an injury which may result in serious physical consequences, it is nevertheless inflicted by words or signs as opposed to actions. Several of the terms denoting slander thus reflect its basis in speech. Both defamation and infamy suggest a diminishment in fame, usually accomplished by means of speech; the etymological root of fame itself is found in speech, deriving from the Greek *phanai*, to speak (*OED*). However, speech must be published or circulated to make an impact; the Indo-European root of fame, *bha*, is also the root of terms related to shining or revealing, such as the Greek *phainein*, "to bring to light" or the English "epiphany."[2] "Slander," which shares its etymological root with "scandal," signifies in similarly double ways. The first sense of the term offered in the *OED* explains slander as "1. The utterance or dissemination of false statements or reports concerning a person, or malicious misrepresentation of his actions, in order to defame or injure him." This seems straightforward enough: slander imputes false crimes against its undeserving target. However, the opposite meaning is also available: "3. Discredit, disgrace, or shame, incurred by or falling upon a person or persons, *esp.* on account of some transgression of the moral law, unworthy action, or misdemeanour; evil name, ill repute, opprobrium." Here slander is not the result of groundless ill-speaking but a true report of one's own ill-doing; in the first case one is an innocent victim, while in the other a deservedly exposed offender. The editors go on to note that the latter definition is "in some cases not clearly separable from sense 1."

Which is precisely the problem. Although the primary understanding of slander in sixteenth-century England defines it as the false imputation of a crime or other shameful behavior/status, this sense is by no means a stable one. The very problem with defamation is its ability to be believed and thus inflict damage on its victim. How is the listener to determine whether the accusation is true or false, if the victim is or is not deserving of ill repute? The actions and intentions of the victim must be investigated in trying to resolve this question, but those of the speaker must be queried as well. Thus the indeterminacy of slander, evidenced in the very definition of the term, raises linguistic, legal and, as I will argue, political problems. However, before turning to the issues the problem specifically engaged for early modern society, I would like to look at the development of defamation in legal history.

According to Roman law, infamy functioned in dual, juxtaposed roles. To defame, *infamare*, someone's reputation made the speaker liable to a suit of *actio iniuriam*:

iniuria was a private crime . . . prosecuted only at the request of the offended person . . . Penalties varied in the course of time from pecuniary reparation

. . . to more severe penalties, such as flogging, scourging, exile, according to the gravity of the injury and the social status of the culprit. In the *actio iniuriam* the plaintiff made his own assessment of the extent of the damages in a sum of money and the judge sentenced the defendant to what seemed to him *bonum et aequum* . . . (Berger 1953: 500, 502)

The law forbade "the doing or saying anything orally or by writing . . . for the purpose of defamation" (Berger 1953: 500). It is interesting to note that defamation was sometimes practiced in the form of a written lampoon (*libellus famosus*) or poem; the latter instance, the *carmen famosum*, was considered one of the graver types of *iniuria* and was punished by deportation (Berger 1953: 562, 381). On the other hand, *infamia* was a condition of ill repute which the state imposed on a guilty party; far from being an offense prosecuted by the courts, it operated as a *punishment* instituted by law to inhibit certain behaviors.

The oldest measure to brand a person as dishonest was the *nota censuria* which was a moral punishment by the censors for misconduct in political or private life . . . The praetorian edict deprived certain persons for moral reasons of the right of appearance in court as advocates or representatives of a party to the trial, or of being represented by another. In particular, persons condemned for crimes or private wrongdoings (*delicta*) were struck by this measure . . . Besides procedural disabilities *infamia* caused other disadvantages such as exclusion from tutorship and denial of the right to obtain a public office or to be an accuser in a criminal trial. (Berger 1953: 500)

Thus, infamy could result from an illegitimate imputation of alleged misbehavior or a judicial condemnation of actual misdeeds.

This dual concept of infamy also manifested itself in English ecclesiastical law (though it is not clear how English law of defamation relates to or is derived from the Roman code [Helmholz 1985: xx–xxiv, xxxiv–xxxvii]). On the one hand, ecclesiastical *infamia*, like Roman law, resulted in "civil and judicial disabilities which followed from the commission of certain acts or the existence of public scandal" (Helmholz 1985: xxi). One so defamed was then liable to canonical purgation; she or "he could be required by a public court of the Church to take a formal oath that he was innocent of the crime and to find compurgators to swear that they believed he had sworn truly" (Helmholz 1985: xxii). On the other hand, a constitution enacted by the Council of Oxford (1222), the *Auctoritate dei patris*, made provision for those who had been wrongfully subjected to the process of compurgation:

We excommunicate all those who, for the sake of hatred, profit, or favour, or for whatever other cause, maliciously impute a crime to any person who is not of ill fame among good and substantial persons, by reason of which purgation at least is [imposed upon] him or he is harmed in some other manner. (Helmholz 1985: xiv)[3]

It is interesting to note that the purgation process, while it could serve to clear the reputation of one defamed, was nevertheless understood as a kind of trial which one was ordered to undergo; it was clearly linked with the notion of rendering a deserving party *infamis*. In contrast, the purpose of the *Auctoritate dei patris* was to protect the innocent from unjust infamy, or defamation.

The ecclesiastical redress for defamation nevertheless imports the tension of just/false accusation in its definition of the injury as the malicious imputation of a *crime*. In a slander case, the possibility always exists that the allegation is true, and that the "victim" of slander is in fact the perpetrator of a crime. In fact, the ecclesiastical definition of slander does not require that the accusation be false.[4] Thus, at least in theory, the positions of plaintiff and defendant could be reversed at any time. However, defamation is not only reversible, it is also reflexive, since each party in effect counter-accuses the other: one is charged with some crime, the other charged with the offense of slander. The ecclesiastical punishment for defamation continues this reflexivity; European canon law suggests, as a possible chastisement, a form of *lex talionis* in which the slanderer would receive the punishment the injured party would have suffered if the accusation were proved true (Helmholz 1985: xvii). The English redress for defamation offers a version of this *lex talionis*; since the effect of the slander was to humiliate the victim, the defamer was similarly exposed to public ridicule. She or he was required, in public, to repent and apologize to the victim: "the evident goal [of this punishment was] the public humiliation of the defamer and the restoration, as far as possible, of the reputation of the person defamed" (Helmholz 1985: xl).

The instability of the definition of defamation as the malicious imputation of a crime has other consequences for legal practice and judicial control, as is evidenced in conflicts over jurisdiction between the ecclesiastical and secular courts.[5] Since the common law did not offer a redress for defamation until the sixteenth century, the ecclesiastical courts heard cases imputing secular as well as ecclesiastical offenses (Helmholz 1985: VI). Because all crimes were considered sins, the ecclesiastical courts could justify that

> "cognizance, examination and correction of every mortal sin", came within [its] jurisdictional reach . . . On that score, bishops might investigate the guilt of a man accused by *infamia* [i.e., a valid charge of wrongdoing] of a secular crime, although punishment of the sinner was reserved for the secular judge. (Helmholz 1985: xxiv)

Thus the possibility existed, even in the case of an alleged defamation (as opposed to one of *infamia*) that the words were true and that the plaintiff of the slander case could become a defendant in a criminal case. However, the converse case was a more common and troubling one; in the fourteenth century the central courts objected that persons who gave evidence for a lawful prosecution within a secular court were being charged with defamation in the ecclesiastical courts. Strikingly, since canon law defined defamation as motivated by malice but did not stipulate that it be false, it was conceivable that a malicious, albeit true, accusation could be considered defamatory. Parliament quickly enacted a statute which prevented this abuse, but a similar problem reappeared during Henry VIII's reign within the common law system. Although it led eventually to the development of a redress for malicious prosecution, the issue was not resolved until late in the sixteenth century (Helmholz 1985: xli–xliii; Baker 1990: 506). The courts' inability to contain slander completely demonstrates not only the imperfect and evolving nature of early modern English law but also the slipperiness of the offense itself.[6]

The instability of slander is further complicated by the vagaries of its development in the common law. For most of the sixteenth century, the majority of slander cases considered by the central law courts allege the false imputation of a secular crime. While this definition is virtually identical to the ecclesiastical one, it differs in the assumption that such an accusation has temporal consequences.[7] The effect of the words spoken is increasingly a concern, as cases come before the courts in which words not imputing a crime clearly resulted in financial loss. Although the common law does not, initially, provide redress for these complaints, by the end of the sixteenth century the scope of the injury has developed to include words which result in demonstrable financial loss. Thus, even imputations of such "spiritual" crimes as unchastity or bastardy, if effecting a temporal loss, would be actionable in the common law (Helmholz 1985: civ–cv). This creates tension in the logic of the redress: is defamation determined by the substance of the words spoken or in terms of the damage resulting from the speech? As Helmholz, a leading historian of English defamation law, notes:

> Regrettably, the older law [in which slander is defined as the imputation of a crime] was not abandoned or brought within new and explicit principles centred around the question of loss. Disputes over whether or not spoken words had imputed a crime continued to fill the reports. They exist alongside the other cases. The result has been the fragmented and unsatisfactory law of libel and slander which has come down to the present day. (Helmholz 1985: cvi)

Thus, by the end of the sixteenth century the common law measured slander both in terms of its content *and* its effect. It was defined as intrinsically harmful, as in the case of words imputing a crime or certain diseases, and contextually injurious, as in the case when temporal loss resulted from the words spoken.[8]

The concern for the effects of words serves to ground defamation in the realm of the material or temporal, moving it out of the ecclesiastical category of the spiritual. While the common law definition was focusing on financial loss, the Star Chamber developed a category of criminal defamation – libel – which measured the crime in terms of its disruption of public order.

> Although redress might be ordered for the victim, the chief concern was with the punishment of sedition on the one hand and of words likely to cause private disorder on the other. (Milsom 1981: 389)

This trend would seem to stabilize defamation by quantifying its consequences: the words cost me this much in income or started a brawl in which this number of people were injured. However, in moving from the ideal to the real, common law defamation began to lose its definitional clarity.[9] When slander is determined by its outcome, the words function in relative rather than absolute terms, since the same speech can have different effects once the context is changed. Thus, emphasizing the effect of defamation allows for contradiction in its definition. When financial damages are the gist of the action, then the words spoken must be false; if the allegation is true, then the subject's actions, and not the speaker's words, bring about monetary loss. However, when breach of the peace determines the actionability of the words, then the truth is immaterial. In fact, one contemporary legal theorist argued that a true allegation, because more painful, is more likely to initiate a dispute than a falsehood (Hudson 1791–2, II: 103). Thus, words can be defamatory whether they are true or false, depending on the consequences.

While the common law development of defamation took its initial form from ecclesiastical redress, it nevertheless distinguished itself, of necessity, from its precursor and competitor.[10] Lacking an authoritative statute or precedent which articulated a definition of defamation, common law lawyers drew their arguments from decisions made in previous cases. Since the redress was essentially a new one in common law, this practice bordered on the solipsistic, which allowed for a certain amount of fluidity and uncertainty. Helmholz argues that this situation promoted legal innovation:

> English lawyers framed their arguments by analogies drawn from previous cases: if actionable there, why not here? If "worthy to be hanged" had been held actionable, should not "bloodsucker" also be actionable? Lawyers could not point to any text like *Auctoritate dei patris* which contained an authoritative statement of the remedy, and this made for easier arguments in favour of expansion. (Helmholz 1985: cv)

This expansion occurred very slowly and within the structure of an essentially conservative system. Even though there is evidence that changes in judicial personnel during the period helped foster change, common law principles exercised a generally restraining influence. Nevertheless, given the case-driven nature of the development of slander law, litigants exerted considerable influence in defining the scope of the redress.[11]

There is one area, however, in which judicial involvement also revealed structural inconsistencies in the determination of slander cases. The rule of construction authorized judges to ascertain the intent and significance of the alleged slander. The *mitior sensus* doctrine construed "ambiguous or doubtful words in the milder sense (*in mitiori sensu*) so that they would not be actionable" (Baker 1990: 501). Helmholz suggests that this policy, which "allowed the judges to deny recovery for slander if any way could be found of interpreting the words in a lenient sense, as imputing no crime," was intended to affirm "the principle that in order to be liable in an action on the case, the speaker must have put his subject in danger of the penalties of the criminal law" (Helmholz 1985: xcii). Opposed to this doctrine was a rule of interpretation "that words were to be taken *in malam partem* when they were malicious and tended to harm the plaintiff" (Helmholz 1985: xciv). Helmholz concludes from this ostensibly contradictory evidence that "probably the most frequently invoked rule of construction was that the words should be taken as they were commonly understood in the place spoken" (Helmholz 1985: xciv). This rule of thumb seems quite reasonable, but its practical application must have given rise to interpretive differences. The judicial problems of determining the guilt or innocence of the plaintiff – or the defendant for that matter, who is either slandered or justly accused of a crime – are hence complicated by the hermeneutic difficulty in deciding if the intent or significance of the imputation constitutes slander.[12]

I turn now to address an important question: to what extent was slander a significant social concern? Heretofore, I have focused on the structural complexities of defamation; I will now explore the problems slander raises when it is put into play within the larger context of early modern English society. Most legal historians agree that actions for slander enjoyed considerable popularity once the redress became established by the middle of the sixteenth century:

> By the 1560s actions on the case for words figure on the plea rolls in sufficient quantity and with sufficient regularity of form to be considered a settled part of the jurisdiction of the royal courts . . . During the remainder of the sixteenth century, the number of cases found increased markedly in King's Bench; somewhat less so in the Common Pleas. (Helmholz 1985: lxxxvi)

The rise in slander litigation[13] occurs during a period when "families were moving up and down in the social and economic scale faster than at any time before the nineteenth and twentieth centuries" (Stone 1967: 22). Attendant on this phenomenon is what Lawrence Stone terms the "cult of reputation":

> One of the most characteristic features of the age was its hyper-sensitive insistence upon the overriding importance of reputation. Many of the punishments of the day, the stocks, the pillory, the apology read out in the market-place, were based upon the theory that public humiliation was a more effective penalty than a swingeing fine. The extraordinary seventeenth-century code of the duel, under which men felt impelled to risk their lives to avenge a casual word, was merely a cancerous growth from the same cells. (Stone 1967: 25)

The inflation of honors that occurred after the accession of James to the throne further exacerbated this sensitivity. While Elizabeth had been too cautious in distributing titles, James erred in the other direction, ultimately allowing the dignity of knighthood to be sold.

By this inflation, by the venal methods of acquisition, and by the lack of care exercised in sifting the origins and standing of would-be purchasers, the respect for the Crown as the fount of honour was weakened, and the hierarchical structure of society was undermined. (Stone 1967: 43)

However, this increase is not so much an index of the corruption of the court as the result of demographic pressures:

The huge expansion in the numbers of men calling themselves gentleman, esquire, knight, baronet, baron, viscount, and earl is not merely the result of the greed and folly of heralds, courtiers, and kings. Even if the heralds had been sea-green incorruptibles, Buckingham and the courtiers men of austere and blameless lives, and King James a man of iron will and an overflowing treasury, a substantial increase in titles must still have taken place. The insatiable demand for status and honour between 1558 and 1641 is proof of the truth of what has been called "Tawney's Law": that the greater the wealth and more even its distribution in a given society, the emptier become titles of personal distinction, but the more they multiply and are striven for. (Stone 1967: 61)

J. A. Sharpe asserts that "few historians who have studied the social attitudes current in early modern England . . . would not agree that considerations of honour, good name, and reputation were of central importance to that society" (Sharpe 1980: 1), and suggests that the concern for reputation appears to run "from the top to very near the bottom of English society in this period" (Sharpe 1980: 3). Whether slander increased as a result of anxiety over reputation brought on by other factors, or if it in fact contributed to this unease, is beyond the scope of my study; however, it is clear that the desire to preserve reputation in early modern England positioned defamation as a central consideration of the period.

This anxiety also appears in contemporary discussions about maintaining authority and order on both the local and national levels. The capacity of discordant words to disrupt the peace or jeopardize the stability of the realm was an increasing concern of the English state by the end of the sixteenth century. In *De pace regis et regni* (1609), a summary of "the great and generall offences of the realme," legal theorist Ferdinando Pulton identifies discordant words first in his list of perils to the peace of the kingdom.

I haue thought it good to begin with the very roote and principall cause of [offenses to the realm], which are Menaces, Threatnings, and other bitter words, beeing as streames gushing out of contentious spirits, and venemous tongues, their naturall fountaines and springheads, from whence do ensue sometimes Assaults, Batteries, Riots, Routs, Unlawfull assemblies, Forces, and Forcible entries: some other times Forgeries, Periuries, and Oppressions: and ofttimes Maihmes, Manslaughters and Murders . . . And we seldome heare of any the said enormities effected, but they tooke their beginnings of menaces, threats, slaunders, or other euill words. (Pulton 1609: B^r–B^v)

Threatening words are represented as a flood, a natural disaster of language whose calamitous effects can barely be avoided. Incitements to physical violence begin with verbal instigations and result in social disruption.

Pulton goes on to show that slander, that is, injurious language not accompanied by immediate physical threat, is a danger equal to "menaces."

There is another foule puddle that ouzeth from the same corrupt gogmire, and distilleth out of a heart likewise infected with malice and enuie, but is deuised and practised by another meane than the former, which is by libelling, secret slandring, or defaming of another: for this priuy backbiter doth not by words impeach his aduersarie in so manifest and turbulent maner, as the cholericke menacer in his furie doth, but seeming to sit quietly in his study, he doth more deeply pinch him, and infixeth a more durable wound into his fame, and credit, than the other boistrous fellow doth into his bodie. (Pulton 1609: B^v)

Although Pulton presents slander as an offense that is also practiced in private, its effects have serious consequences for public order. The English state had long been aware of defamation's capacity to threaten the stability of the kingdom, although not with the same level of concern that it evinces in the sixteenth and seventeenth centuries. During the reign of Edward I, provision was made in 1275 to punish rumors defaming the reputation of a state official in the statute of *scandalum magnatum* – slander of a magnate. Richard II re-enacted the statute in 1379 and defined which officers were to be considered magnates. A statute of 1389 held that disseminators of defamatory stories would be punished if the author could not be found. As these laws protected only a small portion of the society, it is clear that their promulgators did not have as an aim the preservation of the good name of all subjects. These slander statutes were enacted not so much to protect the reputation of the king's officers as to maintain the security of the kingdom (Holdsworth 1927–66, III:409). The statute of 1379 articulates the fear that unless defamation is suppressed, "Debates and slanders might arise betwixt lords [i.e., magnates], or between the lords and the commons . . . and whereof great peril and mischief might come to all the realm, and quick subversion and destruction of the said realm" (Holdsworth 1927–66, III:409 note 5).

Private quarrels touching honor were, as Pulton suggested, also a matter of great concern for society at large. Chief Justice Edward Coke explains the dangers of defamations between private citizens in the case *de Libellis Famosis* (1606).

> Every libel . . . is made either against either a private man, or against a magistrate or public person. *If it be against a private man it deserves a severe punishment*, for although the libel be made against one, yet it incites all those of the same family, kindred, or society to revenge, and so tends *per consequens* to quarrels and breach of the peace, and may be the cause of shedding of blood, and of great inconvenience.[14] (Coke 1907: 251)

This interpretation suggests that where matters of honor are concerned individuals do not exist; familial or societal ties will always obtain, escalating the significance and the damage of the insult. Thus, defamation between two people will necessarily involve disrupting a larger segment of the society.

Part of the threat of slander to the social order is that it attacked one of the primary means of exercising authority: reputation and status to which obedience was owed.

> In Elizabethan and Stuart England, as in almost all settled states, order depended in the last resort less on courts and procedures than on officeholders and personal relationships . . . Prestige not wealth was the principal reward of office. One of the most crucial foundations of order was the sense among the gentry that office was worth undertaking for the reputation it brought . . . But officeholding was a public act which made men peculiarly vulnerable to defamation. (Fletcher 1985: 92–3)

The main arm of early modern law enforcement was the unpaid constables and justices of the peace who performed their duties not only out of a sense of obligation to the state, but also with a desire for increased local standing which office-holding ideally brought. However, if serving as a magistrate could enhance one's reputation, it also made status more vulnerable by placing it more centrally in the public eye. Additionally, chastising neighbors who fell foul of the law and adjudicating conflicts between constituents could expose a public servant's reputation to malicious imputations.

While [the] credit [of a county officer] among his peers might be elevated by their appreciation of his concern for justice, it could also be blotted if it became known or was believed that he abused his authority. His standing among the people could sink if gossip about his conduct, whether malicious or well founded, was allowed to spread unchecked. (Fletcher 1985: 92)

Paradoxically, holding public office simultaneously raised and put in jeopardy one's reputation.

In order to rule effectively, the public servant needed to be vigilant in protecting his reputation not only from the imputations of his subordinates but also from his competitors for office.

Reputation was best advanced by activity and involvement, by the humiliation of rivals that was part and parcel of the desire for rule . . . There was plenty of provocation of rivals in the administrative dealings of this period . . . yet the ambiguities of the code of honour it seems played into the hands of those most adept at underhand behaviour and at sailing close to the wind. Competitive relationships in the government of the shires were not usually swiftly resolved but rather were kept in persistent tension for periods of months or sometimes years. (Fletcher 1985: 93–4)

Defamation was thus both threat to maintaining one's own status and ruling efficacy and a tool with which one could, if used carefully, effect the downfall of a powerful competitor.[15]

If defamation was understood as a potential threat to the peace of the realm, actual treason was often analyzed in terms of slander or sedition. In a Star Chamber discussion of 1599 the Lord Keeper condemns critics of the queen's Irish policy as notorious defamers:

Yett of late are there fownd, some wicked and traitorous p[er]sons (Monsters of men) that w[i]thout regarde of dutie or conscience, and w[i]thout feare of God, or man, cease not in the abundance of their malice, to traduce her Ma[jes]tie, and her direcc[i]on[s] [?] and counselles, and to sclaunder her counsellors and ministers, not only by rayling open speaches, but also by false lying and trayterous libles . . . [S]ome of late have played preachers, and vnder gen[er]all speaches, have vsed such p[ar]ticulaer designacons, as their malicious meaning that appeared to their simplest auditors . . . some other (and those most dangerous of all) doe contriue and publishe false and sedicious libelles, scattering the same in many p[ar]tes of the cittie of London, yea and in her Ma[jes]tes court it self, sclaundering and defaming thereby, sondry p[ar]ticuler p[er]sons, some privie counsellors, some othere her Ma[jes]tes good and faytheful servantes and minsteres, with many false, malicious, and vylanious imputations. But that p[er]happs may seeme light and little; nay they forbeare not to taxe her sacred Ma[jes]tie. (PRO SP 12/273 60^{v}–61^{r})

Critics of royal policy are demonized as monstrous, malicious defamers who operate by means of deception and theatrical impersonation. Even the auditors of such dangerous opinion are accounted as culpable as the "principall Actors" if they do not inform the proper authorities of the libel.

It may be some may thinck that to be hearers or p[re]sent at such sedicious discourses or to knowe of the making and contriving of such libells is a small offence or none at all, but that the fault wil lye wholy vpon the Devisors and Doeres thereof; But lett none be deceaved, for whosoev[er] dothe but *perbere aures*, and doe conceale and not discov[er] such talkeres and discoursers, and such sedicious libellores, hearing or being privie thereof[?] they cannot be deemed, but as maynteyneres and favoureres of the same, and to be punished as severely, as the principall Actors. (PRO SP 12/273: 61^{r})

The seriousness of the threat of defamation in the eyes of the state is starkly emphasized by the Lord Treasurer's comments on the foregoing speech:

These viperous and secrete Libellores doe much more in my opinion deserrue death, then those wch committ open rebellion agaynst the state; for agaynst such as discouer themselves playne and open Rebelles, Princes wth the helpe of their good subiectes, doe speedilie arme themselves, and easilie suppresse them. Agaynst the sword and bullet there is an armour of proofe, yea agaynst the cannon shott their are Bullwarkes and Reumpieres of defence, but agaynst these secrete and sclanderous Libellers there is noe remedy, there is noe resistance; ffor [*sic*] even the most innocent person, and the greatest and iustest king, stand subiect to the venome of his stynge, so as for myne owne opinion I protest, yf there weare a Parliament, I should more willingly give my voyce to establish a lawe of death agaynst them than agaynst the Theife or Murderer. (PRO SP 12/273 64^{r})

The power of defamation lies in its ability to disseminate effectively and anonymously its poison to all members of society, regardless of status. State authority cannot completely control the development and circulation of popular criticism. In the face of this limit to their power, state officials can only disparage, not contain, verbal dissent. In effect, the only recourse against slander is to discredit, that is, to slander, it.

However, if imputations against the state threatened its stability, public humiliation could nevertheless be employed by the state as a particularly effective means of discipline in early modern England. In a 1596 Star Chamber fraud case, the defendants were found guilty and sentenced to be imprisoned, fined twenty pounds, and whipped four times around the city. They were also to be placed in the pillory with papers attached which literally wrote the crime on the perpetrators so their disgrace could be read by all. To this humbling and harsh punishment William Burghley suggested an explicitly theatrical addition: "The Lord Treasurer 'would haue those y^{t} make the playes to make a Comedie hereof, & to acte it wth these names'" (Hawarde 1894: 48). There is no evidence that Burghley's proposal was acted upon, but the suggestion shows that he clearly appreciated the capacity of a play to expose the defendants and warn others by its example. All public punishment – from the scaffold to the pillory – operated on the premise that the humiliation of the criminal acted as a future deterrent both for the criminal as well as witnesses of the event. This calculated theatrical exposure served to disgrace both the offender and his offense in the eyes of the public.

To the extent that punishment worked to make the criminal infamous, it essentially functioned as slander. In fact, the English legal system relied on types of institutionalized defamation in both the punishment and the indictment of criminals. Justices of the peace regularly depended on reports from local inhabitants to inform them of crimes committed. In turn, the JPs were expected to give these petitions to the grand jury who would hand down an indictment if they determined the accusation was true (Harding 1973: 76). However, for misdemeanors both the plaintiff or the government could circumvent the grand jury's intervention (Baker 1990: 578). And either could

> [order] arrest and trial on the *information* of private persons, without getting a grand jury to confirm the charges . . . In early Stuart times an average county might have as many as twelve professional informers working in cooperation with the clerk of the peace, each bringing twenty or so prosecutions to quarter-session, and some directing rudimentary detective agencies. (Harding 1973: 76–7)

Thus the system at its most fundamental level was based on the criminal accusations of one private citizen by another, with cases brought to trial without the more objective deliberations of a disinterested grand jury.[16] By the end of the seventeenth century the process was emended by Parliament in response to complaints that "the procedure could too easily be abused in bringing unfounded prosecutions" (Baker 1979: 418–19).

One's reputation or standing in the community was of the utmost importance when authorities were searching out suspects. Bad fame was considered evidence enough to suspect someone of a crime.

> A rather more dubious proceeding than information, though it had ancient roots, was trial upon "record". It was in part an extension of the old principle that notoriety was adequate to accuse a man – and even to condemn him. (Harding 1973: 77)

If someone possessing a bad reputation was in fact deserving of it, then it was logical that he or she be questioned when a crime was committed. However, while the informations and imputations brought against a suspect could be true, they could also be motivated by personal hatred, a desire to harass or vex, or a malicious impulse to slander.

Similarly, the state's reliance on various forms of defamation could just as easily work against, instead of for, its interests. In cases of guilt by notoriety, infamous accusations could be turned against the state.

> J.P.s sometimes had authority to arrest on suspicion . . . [T]he analogous king's witness of rebellion was no less than incontrovertible, so that it was found politically convenient to condemn rebels on the king's record . . . The families of the noble victims of this doctrine that notoriety to the king equalled condemnation, naturally claimed that it was contrary to law; and it was certainly dangerous. The practice was . . . turned against the Crown, which found its ministers, from the end of the fourteenth century right on to the eighteenth, being impeached by parliament on the same basis of "notorious crimes." (Harding 1973: 77–8)

The cruelty and humiliation of public executions could likewise redound to the infamy of the state and not the criminal. Michel Foucault's observations on the reversibility of an execution's intended effect, though made with regard to conditions in eighteenth-century France, are corroborated by events in early modern England.[17]

> In these executions, which ought to show only the terrorizing power of the prince, there was a whole aspect of the carnival, in which rules were inverted, authority mocked and criminals transformed into heroes. The shame was turned round; the courage, like the tears and the cries of the condemned, caused offence only to the law. (Foucault 1979: 61; see also 58–69 *passim*)

The popularity of Foxe's *Actes and Monuments* demonstrates the extent to which public opinion could side with the "criminal" (as martyr) against the popish state.[18] Likewise, Elizabeth's displeasure over the execution of Mary Queen of Scots, following her signing of the death warrant, indicates her desire to dissociate herself from the event to avoid popular, though in this case foreign, disapproval; "In Scotland . . . libels were set up in the streets against James and his Anglophil ministers, and odious epigrams on 'Jezebel, that English whore'" (Neale 1957: 288–92). The execution of the inordinately popular Earl of Essex was privately performed within the Tower grounds to avoid eliciting sympathy amongst his supporters. In spite of this precaution, Essex's executioner was almost mobbed on leaving the Tower and ballads singing Essex's praises appeared immediately after his death (Bowen 1956: 160–2). Thus, the state's use of slander, specifically dramatic public exposures, relied for its success on the very people such spectacles were meant to control, and upon whose acquiescence it could not depend.[19]

Nevertheless defamation, for all its instability, offered too valuable a mechanism of criminalization to be eschewed. The employment of false accusations against the enemies of the state, in the form of propaganda, provided an excellent tool for justifying royal authority. State trials, while often presenting legitimate charges against traitors, bristled with calumny when the accused were hapless victims of factional enmity at court. Sir Walter Ralegh provides a striking and frequently discussed example; his case is particularly interesting because of the contradictory nature of the charges against him.[20] Ralegh's conviction in 1603 of involvement in a plot "to kill the king, place Arabella Stuart on the throne, and make peace with Spain" (Greenblatt 1973: 114) was a very odd and improbable charge given his legendary hatred for the Spanish. Ralegh himself commented on this irony in a letter to his wife:

> all my services, hazards, and expenses for my country, plantings, discoveries, fights, councils, and whatsoever else, malice hath now covered over. I am now made an enemy and traitor by the word of an unworthy man [Cobham, his accuser]; he that proclaimed me to be a partaker of his vain imaginations, notwithstanding the whole course of my life hath approved the contrary. (quoted in Goodman 1839: 94)

In fact, the prosecution had no hard evidence, as Karen Cunningham points out in her analysis of the trial, and was forced to proceed via defamatory imputations (Cunningham 1992: 334–8). Dudley Carleton, in an often quoted letter reporting on the trial, comments on the slanderous nature of prosecution in contrast to Ralegh's admirable response to it:

And so well he shifted all advantages that were taken against him, that were not *fama malum gravius quam res*, and an ill name, half-hanged in the opinion of all men, he had been acquitted. (quoted in David Jardine 1847: 466)

Here, bad fame is more weighty than any deed allegedly committed; Attorney-General Edward Coke, who three years later as Chief Justice writes against the dangerous power of defamation, secured a guilty verdict against Ralegh by means of what amounts to slander.

The irony does not end here. Ralegh, though convicted of treason, was reprieved because, as Cunningham points out, "It would have been a political blunder to execute Ralegh on the Spanish issue while seeking reconciliation with Spain" (Cunningham 1992: 346). Ralegh was held in the Tower, officially "dead," until his release in 1616 when he was ordered to lead an expedition in search of gold in Guiana. When Ralegh's forces were defeated in an unexpected battle with a Spanish settlement on the Orinoco, he returned to England a ruined, impoverished and newly doomed man. While the trip had been supported by the anti-Spanish faction at court, and had been intended as a hostile action, Ralegh bore the brunt of the king's displeasure at this conflict with Spain, at this point England's ostensible ally (Stephen 1899: 61–2). The old indictment against Ralegh, that he conspired with Spain to oust James from his throne, is carried out, without retrial, in order to punish his recent aggression against the Spanish. Ralegh, originally convicted for colluding with the Spanish, is executed for attacking them fourteen years later.[21]

In effect, the use of propaganda in treason trials turns state opinion about slander on its head; while official remarks about slander are condemnatory, the state has no qualms about using what is in effect slander to discredit its own enemies. This is sharply illustrated in Henry VIII's reversal in the Second Act of Succession in which he permits slanders against Anne Boleyn and Elizabeth formerly forbidden in the First Act of Succession.

the kings most roiall maiestie, most gratiouslie considering, that diuers and manie of his most louing and obedient subiects now latelie after the beginning of the present parlement, haue spoken . . . [etc.] against the said vnlawfull mariage, solemnized betweene his highnesse and the said ladie Anne, and to the preiudice, slander, disturbance, and derogation thereof, but also to the perill, slander and disherison of the ladie Elizabeth the kings daughter illegitimat borne vnder the same mariage, and to the let disturbance and interruption of the said ladie Elizabeth to the title of the crowne . . . Which words, dooings . . . albeit they proceeded of no malice, but vpon true and iust grounds . . . yet neuerthelesse the kings said subiects might heereafter happen to be impeached, troubled and vexed for such their words, dooings, acts . . . The kings highnesse therefore of his most bountifull mercie and benignitie is pleased and contented that it be enacted . . . that all and singular his louing subiects, which haue spoken . . . against [the marriage, Anne or Elizabeth], or to anie of their slanders, perils or disherisons . . . shall be freelie and cleerelie pardoned, discharged, and released by authoritie of this act, of all those and such treasons and misprisions of treasons aboue mentioned. (28 H.VIII c.7 746)

Strikingly, the order acknowledges that critical speech against Anne and Elizabeth poses a threat to them, and that such critics might be prosecuted for this offense; while still acknowledging such criticism as a transgression, the Act pardons it. Thus, while attempting to define defamation in absolute terms, the courts and councilors actually use and respond to it in relative terms; the political climate, and not the truth of the speech, determines whether language is defamatory or not. Maintenance of peace, that is, retaining the current political order, finally determines what language is transgressive and what is not. This understanding of language calls into question, if only theoretically, a stable, objective concept of "truth."

Poets, like rulers, faced a similar struggle over problems of truth and falsehood in their vocation. While clearly dealing in fictions, poets nevertheless claimed access to a higher truth untainted by political corruption because motivated by virtue, not ambition. In Book I of *The Arte of English Poesie* George Puttenham gives an "historical" account of the function of poetry. Its first role was to praise the gods; its second was not, as one might suppose, to praise good men, but to correct vice. The purpose of "Poesie *Dramatick* reprehensive" was to foster virtue and order, and thus promote the aims of the state. Dramatic satire was "the first and most bitter inuectiue against vice and vicious men" (Puttenham 1936: 31). The poets of the time disguised themselves as "Satyres" or "Siluans," "as if the gods of the woods . . . should appear and recite those verses of rebuke" (Puttenham 1936: 31). Comedy and tragedy were developed as more persuasive means of correcting abuses; instead of a dramatic narration, the characters of the plot represented the action themselves, creating a more verisimilar, and thus convincing, effect.

However, while comedies "debated the matters of the world, sometimes of [the poets'] priuate affaires, sometimes of their neighbours," tragedies exposed corrupt tyrants, "their miserable ends painted out in playes and pageants, to shew the mutabilitie of fortune, and the iust punishment of God in reuenge of a vicious and euill life" (Puttenham 1936: 32–3). Puttenham does not directly sanction criticism of living princes; he insists that tragedy concern itself with their behavior only after their deaths. Nevertheless, in the section on the praise of princes, he suggests a slightly different perspective. Rulers, because they are "of greater moment," must conform to a higher standard of virtue than "any inferior sort of men."

> Wherefore the Poets being in deede the trumpetters of all praise and also of slaunder (not slaunder, but well deserued reproch) were in conscience & credit bound next after the diuine praises of the immortall gods, to yeeld a like ratable honour to all such amongst men, as most resembled the gods by excellencie of function. (Puttenham 1936: 35)

Puttenham deliberately permits his first thought, "slaunder," to remain alongside his afterthought, "well deserued reproch," which serves to redefine the former. Aware that contemporary opinion equated reproaching the prince with slander, Puttenham tries to make the case that poetic correction is justified by precedent. Thus, according to its "history," while dramatic poetry can assist the state in reproving vice, it also maintains the ability to criticize the state.[22]

However, despite professions that poetic criticism of viciousness, including that of the state, is warranted, poetry cannot escape charges of slanderous intent. Doggerel rhyme, ballads and satire become such popular expressions of detraction that defamation is increasingly associated with poetry. This connection is so strong by the beginning of the seventeenth century that Chief Justice Edward Coke can define a libel as "an epigram, rhyme, or other writing" (Coke 1907: 250), continuing a trend developed in the previous century which associated seditious words and rumors with "rime [and] ballad" (23 Eliz.c.2). Satire was an even more obvious outlet for the defamatory impulse. The Bishop's Ban of 1599, which prohibited the publication of specific satires among other works, was clearly interested in limiting the slanderous effects of contemporary references found in these poems (McCabe 1981: 191–3).

Theatrical impersonation is also understood as a form of defamation, a function which contemporary plays themselves acknowledge.

Consider, for example, Ulysses' complaint about Achilles' theatrical slanders in *Troilus and Cressida*:

> The great Achilles, whom opinion crowns,
> The sinew and the forehand of our host,
> Having his ear full of his airy fame,
> Grows dainty of his worth, and in his tent
> Lies mocking our designs: with him Patroclus
> . . .
> Breaks scurril jests,
> And with ridiculous and awkward action,
> Which, slanderer, he imitations calls,
> He pageants us. Sometime, great Agamemnon,
> Thy topless deputation he puts on;
> . . . like a strutting player, whose conceit
> Lies in his hamstring . . . (I.iii.141–5, 147–53)

It is striking to note that Achilles' sense of his own fame is cited here as motivating his desire to defame others. Hamlet also makes oblique reference to scandalous stage impersonations in the discussion about the boys' company (II.ii.335–58). Hamlet himself makes use of a type of theatrical impersonation, via a performance of *The Murder of Gonzago*; in staging an analogous crime, he attempts to expose his uncle's murder of his father.

Contemporary legal thought identified theatrical impersonation of actual people, especially figures of state, as slander, which distinguished it rhetorically from the state's own practice of humiliating exposure. William Hudson includes a discussion of it in his *Treatise of the Court of Star Chamber* in the chapter on "Libelling and Scandalous Words":

> Libels are of several kinds; either by scoffing at the person of another in rhyme or prose, or by the personating him, thereby to make him ridiculous. (Hudson 1791–2, II: 100)

In May 1601 the Privy Council ordered an investigation of a report that

> certaine players [in Middlesex] . . . do represent upon the stage in their interludes the persons of some gentlemen of good desert and quallity that are yet alive under obscure manner, but yet in such sorte as all the hearers may take notice both of the matter and the persons that are meant thereby. (Chambers 1923, IV: 332)

The Council ordered the county justices of the peace to forbid the performance of the play because it clearly had not been "perused and allowed" by the appropriate authorities and thus could "minister . . . occasion of offence or scandall" (Chambers 1923, IV: 332).

In his review of libel cases, Hudson offers an example of dramatic defamation – "The personating of the earl of Lincoln in a play" (Hudson 1791–2, II: 101) – that was successfully redressed through appropriate legal channels. Most of the documents related to *Lincoln* v. *Dymock* are missing from the Public Record Office, but one of the depositions which remains provides an apparently thorough account of the play (PRO STAC 5 L34/47). The Star Chamber records reveal a prodigious number of cases in which both Lincoln and Edward Dymock are named. In this instance Dymock, a neighbor of the earl, was charged with producing a play in August 1601 in which Lincoln is portrayed as being carried off by the devil. Lincoln is ridiculed further when he is named heir in the fool's will and inherits the latter's wooden dagger. Dymock insured his play an audience by inviting neighbors to a venison feast, after which the skit was performed. His intent was clearly to discredit and humiliate the earl by means of theatrical slander. The Star Chamber recognized the threat of this instance of unauthorized theatrical criticism and, according to Hudson, severely punished the play's perpetrators.[23]

An infamous example from the public theater of the threat of even a veiled theatrical impersonation is the staging of *Richard II* (presumably Shakespeare's) during the Essex rebellion (February 1601). William Lambarde's now familiar account of Elizabeth's remarks (August 1601) on the performance indicates that she understood the implied menace of this attempt to cast her in the role of the monarch deposed by a popular nobleman.[24] The April 1601 proclamation offering a reward for information about authors of "libels . . . tending to the slander of our royal person and state" would have included unauthorized dramatic representations as well as written and verbal attacks (Hughes and Larkin 1964–9, III: 233). Even before the 1601 uprising, Jonson was required to excise the climax of *Every Man Out of His Humour* because it staged a confrontation, and a flattering one at that, of the queen and a satirist (Barish 1981: 137).

In response to this association of their medium with slander, poets counter with strategies similar to the state's. Accusations that poetry is defamatory are themselves branded malicious and slanderous, while the criticisms that poets make about the status quo are justified as enlightened and salutary. Poetry sets up just such another model of valid criticism versus malicious slander with regard to its own discursive practice.

In the course of the sixteenth and seventeenth centuries, slander develops as an central, powerful, and unstable concern for most segments of English society (Sharpe 1980: 3). Anxiety over reputation made verbal public humiliation an effective tool of the state, but the slipperiness of defamation made it impossible to control; thus it could be wielded as an equally dangerous weapon against the state. Its close association with poetry demands not only an investigation of political and social significance of slander for early modern literature but also of the literary and linguistic import of defamation on English politics and culture. In the following chapters I explore the ways in which three poets represent their relationship to authority in the context of contemporary concerns about defamation. Rather than imagining this relation as one in which the ruler or state officials exercise a censoring function to which the poet must adapt, Spenser, Jonson and Shakespeare present poet figures who employ accusations of defamation to delegitimate official criticism of their work and to advance a critique of state-sponsored slander.

2 Allegories of defamation in *The Faerie Queene* Books IV–VI

The Legend of Friendship, the first book of the second installment of *The Faerie Queene*, opens by taking the perspective of a critic of the poet's work in what appears to be a self-criticism. Here "kingdomes causes . . . affaires of state" and virtue itself are presented as antithetical to the false allurements of love that the poet takes as his subject. The minister of state authoritatively judges and rejects "vaine poemes weeds" which lead to folly frail youth "that better were in vertues discipled" (IV. Proem 1). However, the second stanza of this book reveals the injustice of this allegation by rejecting the judgment of the critic; culpability now lies with the speaker of this false imputation rather than with his victim.

> Such ones ill iudge of loue, that cannot loue,
> Ne in their frosen hearts feele kindly flame:
> For thy they ought not thing vnknowne reproue,
> Ne naturall affection faultless blame. (IV. Proem 2)

Love is the root "of honor and all vertue," and poetry, in taking it as its subject, promotes, rather than undermines, virtuous discipline. Spenser brilliantly aligns himself with the example of Elizabeth, the queen whose rhetoric often justified her rule by the love she bore her subjects and who managed the factions at her court by styling them as suitors for her affection, to ballast his defense of love poetry. The "rugged forhead" may have foresight regarding state concerns, but he is rejected as one of the "Stoicke censours" (IV. Proem 3.9) who misunderstands love's relation to virtue and hence cannot serve as a sufficient audience for the poem. Here, the censor's disapproval of a text does not result in the suppression of the work, but in the questioning of the critic's ability to judge, that is to say censure, the poem correctly. The censor, not the poet is silenced here:

> To such therefore I do not sing at all,
> But to that sacred Saint my soueraigne Queene
> . . .
> To her I sing of loue, that loueth best,
> And best is lou'd of all aliue I weene:
> To her this song most fitly is addrest,
> The Queene of loue, and Prince of peace from heauen blest.
> (IV.Proem 4)

Elizabeth's affiliations with love and peace, both in religious and temporal contexts, make her the perfect reader for the poem,[1] while the high aims of the poet make this the perfect poem for her to "reade . . . often" (IV. Proem 5.9).

Without explicitly alluding to defamation, these opening stanzas set up the exploration of slander which runs through the latter three books of *The Faerie Queene*. They present the problem of how to negotiate and invalidate criticisms of poetry made by the state, that is, to render them mere slanders, without implicating the queen whose approval Spenser seeks to create and secure. As "Prince of peace" Elizabeth is concerned with establishing an orderly and settled realm. Official rhetoric of the period concurs with Spenser's representation of slander as disrupting at all levels the important bonds that hold society together. By demonstrating the poet's concern for slander, and his efficacy in silencing it, Spenser intends to represent himself in the ensuing books as a valuable servant to the state. However, as he increasingly senses himself to be the victim of state criticism, he resorts to charging the state with slander as a means of deflecting and dismissing its censure.

If, in the Legend of Friendship, poetry is linked with love as harmony which promotes a settled state, slander appears as the most serious threat to this concord; while words are ideally constitutive of public order, they also have the capacity to destabilize that order. Ate embodies the disruption such words pose to the status quo; she is the

> mother of debate
> And all dissention, which doth dayly grow
> Amongst fraile men, that many a publike state
> And many a priuate oft doth ouerthrow. (IV.i.19)

Like the speakers of "bitter words" Pulton deplores (see chapter I), Ate foments discord by using speech to undermine settled relations on local and national levels. While her sphere of influence encompasses both the domestic and the political, the disruptions she effects in either realm have serious consequences for society at large. She is eager to promote and exacerbate arguments which could lead to violence, and does so by means of lies and slander. She sows

> The seedes of euill wordes, and factious deedes;
> Which when to ripenesse due they growen arre,
> Bring foorth an infinite increase, that breedes
> Tumultuous trouble and contentious iarre,
> The which most often end in bloudshed and in warre. (IV.i.25)

Ate "was borne of hellish brood, / And by infernall furies nourished" (IV. 26); her victims' "feood" is her "food" and she has multiple tongues. She is characterized by doubleness and destruction:

> Als as she double spake, so heard she double,
> With matchlesse eares deformed and distort,
> Fild with false rumors and seditious trouble,
> Bred in assemblies of the vulgar sort,
> That still are led with euery light report
> ...
> vnequall were her handes twaine,
> That one did reach, the other pusht away,
> That one did make the other mard againe,
> And sought to bring all things vnto decay
> ...
> For all her studie was and all her thought,
> How she might ouerthrow the things that Concord wrought.
> (IV.i.28–9)

Rumor and sedition invert and reverse the various bonds that hold society together; they are the means by which Ate aspires to disrupt the established order.[2]

What is the antidote to the serious peril disruptive speech poses to social accord? If discord finds its origins in hell and serves to work confusion in this world, only "a God or godlike man" (IV.ii.1) can quell it. In this case, the poet is this quasi-divine being "Such as was *Orpheus*, that when strife was growen / Amongst those famous ympes of Greece, did take / His siluer Harpe in hand, and shortly friends them make" (IV.ii.1).[3] David, the composer of the Psalms, is also cited as an example; he, like Orpheus, was a harpist. However, if the soothing quality of music is being emphasized here, its verbal or poetic aspect is still crucial: "Such Musicke is wise words with time concented, / To moderate stiffe minds, disposd to striue" (IV.ii.2). The wise content of words set in meter can similarly harmonize discordant parties. Discourse that has the power to disrupt can be countered by words with the power to heal.

Another figure of disruptive language in Book IV is Sclaunder, whose representation apparently ignores the etymological paradox of her name in asserting that her victims are by definition innocent and virtuous:

> Her nature is all goodnesse to abuse,
> And causelesse crimes continually to frame,
> With which she guiltlesse persons may accuse,
> And steale away the crowne of their good name;
> Ne euer Knight so bold, ne euer Dame
> So chast and loyall liu'd, but she would striue
> With forged cause them falsely to defame . . . (IV.viii.25)

This description closely follows the contemporary legal definition of slander in its most general form: the false imputation of crimes. Sclaunder is represented as motivated by another common attribute of defamation, malice:

> For she was stuft with rancour and despight
> Vp to the throat, that oft with bitternesse
> It forth would breake, and gush in great excesse . . . (IV.viii.24)

Defamation functions by creating opportunities for misinterpretation, the virtuous are "lewdly miscall[ed]" with "leasings" (IV.viii.24) which are then believed by others.

However, while Spenser offers a traditional representation of slander as the maliciously motivated false imputation of a crime, he also suggests the notion that her words are almost without content:

> Her words were not, as common words are ment,
> T'expresse the meaning of the inward mind,
> But noysome breath, and poysnous spirit sent
> From inward parts, with canred malice lind
> And breathed forth with blast of bitter wind;
> Which passing through the eares, would pierce the hart,
> And wound the soule it selfe with griefe vnkind:
> For like the stings of Aspes, that kill with smart,
> Her spightfull words did pricke, and wound the inner part.
> (IV.viii.26)

Defamation originates in the inward parts and attacks the inner part;

it operates less like discourse and more like a physical assault of "noysome breath, and . . . blast of bitter wind" (26). In contrast to "common" speech, slander does not represent the mind's true intent, which raises the possibility that it represents nothing at all. It has no referent, which makes it infinitely referential and particularly susceptible to attempts of attribution: the pressure of the mind to make sense out of words is increased when no obvious sense is intended.[4]

This hermeneutic structure of a non-referential statement providing an opportunity for misreading presents a more benign example of slander in contrast to the threat posed by Ate. While Sclaunder may be motivated by spite, her words cause little damage and are ultimately meaningless. Arthur, Amoret and Aemylia pass away from her house with only minor internal injuries, leaving Sclaunder to blunt her tongue on inattentive objects:

> At last when they were passed out of sight,
> Yet she did not her spightfull speach forbeare.
> But after them did barke, and still backbite,
> Though there were none her hatefull words to heare:
> . . .
> So she them seeing past the reach of eare,
> Against the stones and trees did rayle anew,
> Till she had duld the sting, which in her tongs end grew. (IV.viii.36)

Spenser is troubled not so much by Sclaunder, although her railings vex Arthur and his party, as by a "misregard[ing] . . . rash witted" reader "Whose looser thought will lightly be misled, / These gentle Ladies will misdeeme too light, / For thus conuersing with this noble Knight" (IV.viii.29). While the three noble characters of this episode experience pain from Sclaunder's attacks, they are the only ones who hear her accusations; their reputations are immune from damage as long as readers fail to believe her imputations. However, misregarding readers magnify slander through false interpretations that result in false imputations; the more serious damage inflicted by defamation in *The Faerie Queene* is wrought by the misreader *of* the poem, and not the misspeaker *in* the poem. This reader suggests that the poet defames his own characters by placing them in a compromising situation. Spenser repels the misregarding reader's attack by turning to the notion of contemporary decay and showing that the degradation the reader perceives in others results from living in a fallen society that can no longer understand the virtue of antique times (IV.29–33). First cast as the author of slanders, the poet returns the accusation by demonstrating that he is the victim of slanders. Rather than being censored and silenced by his critics, Spenser turns the tables in identifying them as the source of disruptive speech.

Spenser extends this exploration of the threat of slander to the state in relation to poetry in Book V. The "mayden Queene" Mercilla defines herself not only through her bounty and grace, but by "strongly beat[ing] downe / The malice of her foes, which her enuy, / And at her happinesse do fret and frowne" (V.viii.17). While the Souldan and his wife Adicia, the embodiment of injustice, pursue numerous methods of undermining Mercilla's rule, the impulses which motivate them are ones traditionally linked with defamation. When she and her husband are ultimately foiled by Arthur and Artegall, Adicia metamorphoses into a tiger whose description prefigures that of the Blatant Beast, the slander animal. She is likened to

> a mad bytch, when as the franticke fit
> Her burning tongue with rage inflamed hath,
> Doth runne at randon, and with furious bit
> Snatching at euery thing, dothe wreake her wrath
> On man and beast, that commeth in her path. (V.viii.49)

Slander becomes the epitome of injustice gone wild. Upon arriving at Mercilla's court, the two knights find Awe guarding the entrance

> To keepe out guyle, and malice, and despight,
> That vnder shew oftimes of fayned semblance,
> Are wont in Princes courts to worke great scath and hindrance.
> (V.ix.22)

Of all the various threats that face the monarch and her court, again defamatory motives, "malice and despight," are emphasized as most dangerous. Malfont appears directly after this passage to illustrate the successful silencing of this menace. Counter-intuitively, Spenser seems to concur with legal and popular association of poetry with slandering the state in the Bon/Malfont episode (V.ix), but an examination of this passage demonstrates that the poet represents this connection only to discredit it.[5] Malfont is judged guilty of a trespass for which he is punished by having his tongue nailed to a post:

For that therewith he falsely did reuyle,
And foule blaspheme that Queene for forged guyle,
Both with bold speaches, which he blazed had,
And with lewd poems, which he did compyle;
For the bold title of Poet bad
He on himselfe had ta'en, and rayling rymes had sprad. (v.ix.25)

His first crime is against the queen insofar as he accuses her of fraud. However, he also seems to be committing an offense against poetry by taking on the title of a bad poet, simultaneously distorting and usurping the true poet's role. He suffers corporal punishment for his crime against the state, but the change his name undergoes penalizes his offense against poetry. As Bonfont, this figure represented the true poet, the fount of virtue; Hamilton juxtaposes the debased poet's characterization as "a welhed / Of euill words" to Spenser's description of Chaucer as "well of English vndefyled" (note to stanza 26, 592). But in perverting the role of good poet he ceases to be one:

but *bon* that once had written bin,
Was raced out, and *Mal* was now put in
. . .
Eyther for th'euill, which he did therein,
Or that he likened was to a welhed
Of euill words, and wicked sclaunders by him shed. (v.ix.26)

Malfont's only connection with poetry is that he abuses it; the *mal* replaces the *bon* in his name for the evil "which he did therein," that is, for the perversion of poetry whose proper function is "True vertue to aduance" (v.iii.3).

In spite of the ways in which defamation is represented as antithetical and antagonistic to the queen and her court, it nevertheless has value for use against the state's enemies. The trial of Duessa illustrates subtly but quite powerfully that slander also benefits a ruler. Poetry's affiliations with infamy are similarly hinted at in this positive context. As attorney general, Zele's expertise lies not only in his "deepe reach, / And rare in-sight" but also in his ability to "well . . . charme his tongue and time his speach / To all assayes" (v.ix.39), a reference which resonates with the concordant powers attributed earlier to poetry: "Such Musicke is wise words with time concented, / To moderate stiffe minds, disposed to striue" (iv.ii.2). In setting up the context for the trial, the text suggests that Duessa's own actions have brought deserved disgrace upon her; she "with foule abuse did marre" her "great countenance and place" (v.ix.38). However, Zele's accusations, while presumably true, nevertheless suggest a manipulation of the facts to sway the judge against the accused, and result in a defamation of the latter:

> Strongly did *Zele* her haynous fact enforce,
> And many other crimes of foule defame
> Against her brought, to banish all remorse,
> And aggrauate the horror of her blame. (v.ix.43)

While Zele brings many respectable witnesses to help plead his case against Duessa, she succeeds in calling defendants of her own which incline Mercilla toward her. As a counter-strategy,

> He gan t'efforce the euidence anew,
> And new accusements to produce in place:
> He brought forth that old hag of hellish hew,
> The cursed *Ate*, brought her face to face,
> Who priuie was, and partie in the case:
> She, glad of spoyle and ruinous decay,
> Did her appeach, and to her more disgrace,
> The plot of all her practise did display,
> And all her traynes, and all her treasons forth did lay. (v.ix.47)

On the face things, Zele's calling Ate to the stand makes sense; she is a co-conspirator and can give solid evidence against her partner in crime. However, Ate herself is not being prosecuted, even though she "priuie was, and partie in the case"; in fact, the very qualities that make Ate so disruptive of social bonds are here employed by the prosecutor to sever any connection that Duessa's pleaders (including Pittie and Griefe) might have established between the judge and the accused. Zele calls forth a number of other crimes, including Sedition, to testify against Duessa. The obvious sense of the allegory suggests that her own actions are witness against her, that she brings on her indictment as a result of her own crimes. But shimmering behind this reading is the notion that the state itself employs these crimes, or imputes them to her through the slanderous agency of Ate. In his efforts to produce Duessa's guilt, Zele paradoxically aligns himself with the very crimes he seeks to condemn in her.

James I, in an oft-cited complaint to Burghley, clearly understood this allegory to be a defamation of his mother Mary, Queen of Scots

(Spenser 1977: 595). However, he faults Spenser, not Elizabeth who perpetrated the charges against Mary, for dishonoring both him and his mother.[6] The passage serves the interests of the English state in representing Duessa/Mary in a negative light and in painting a very positive picture of Mercilla/Elizabeth's reluctant judgment. The final judgment against Duessa is so tactfully represented that the death sentence is never articulated and her execution can only be inferred through Mercilla's "yeelding the last honour to her wretched corse" (v.x.4). The poem successfully deflects criticisms or slanders of Elizabeth's actions – James complains about Spenser, not Elizabeth – by emphasizing her mercy toward the accused. Nevertheless, James' accusation neither hinders Spenser's ability to turn his poem to the defense of his queen from slanders in response to Mary's death nor to represent official slanders against Mary.

However, existing simultaneously with this positive representation of state–poet relations regarding slander is a more sinister view that the state is no longer using slander against enemies but, increasingly, against its most loyal servants: Sir Walter Ralegh, Arthur, Lord Grey, and the poet himself. A return to Book IV is necessary to develop this claim. A fuller exploration of the context of the Sclaunder episode develops the problem of ambiguous culpability in slander in relations between the state and its servants. The narrative begins with Lust attacking Amoret under circumstances that will be repeated in Book VI when the Blatant Beast attacks Serena:

> faire Amoret, of nought affeard,
> Walkt through the wood, for pleasure, or for need;
> When suddenly behind her backe she heard
> One rushing forth out of the thickest weed,
> That ere she backe could turne to taken heed,
> Had vnawares her snatched vp from ground. (IV.vii.4)

The allegory of this episode is tantalizingly equivocal: is Amoret the object of male lust or is she overcome by her own feelings of lust? When Belphoebe comes upon Timias tending Amoret's wound – the wound he inflicted in trying to free her from Lust – is she looking at a display of innocent tenderness for a wounded creature, or an intimate caress? James Bednarz suggests the possibility that the poet leaves this episode ambiguous in order to placate his two patrons who are in conflict in the allegory: Belphoebe/Elizabeth and Timias/Ralegh. The historical incident underlying this story is Ralegh's banishment from court after eloping with Elizabeth Throckmorton, one of the queen's maids-in-waiting. Bednarz argues that Spenser ultimately comes down on Ralegh's side: "The reconciliation of Timias and Belphoebe . . . does not distribute blame equally between Ralegh and Elizabeth. Instead, it contradicts the imputation of guilt leveled against Ralegh and criticizes the queen for her rashness" (Bednarz 1983: 65). Belphoebe is described as viewing the scene between Amoret and Timias with a "sodaine glauncing eye," on the basis of which she develops a false interpretation: "Her noble heart with sight thereof was fild / With deepe disdaine, and great indignity" (IV.vii.36). Her hasty conclusion becomes a filter through which she misreads the situation; once she has made up her mind, Belphoebe can no longer see the couple as anything other than sexually engaged. Her disdain reads like blinding jealousy, and prevents her from formulating another explanation for the incident: "Is this the faith, she said, and said no more, / But turnd her face, and fled away for euermore" (vii.36).

Belphoebe's reading of the Timias and Amoret encounter results in dishonor for the squire:

> And euermore, when he did grace entreat,
> And framed speaches fit for his behoofe,
> Her mortall arrowes she at him did threat,
> And forst him backe with fowle dishonor to retreat. (IV.vii.37)

Thomas Roche sees the Belphoebe and Timias episode as an allegory of honor (Roche 1964: 143).[7] Timias embodies honor, as the etymology of his name – derived from the Greek *timios*, "honored" – suggests; when he is dishonored, essentially defamed, by Belphoebe, he in effect ceases to exist.[8] When Belphoebe later happens upon the "UnTimias," she fails to recognize him and the cause of his plight:

> But wondred much at his so selcouth case,
> And by his persons secret seemlyhed
> Well weend, that he had beene some man of place,
> Before misfortune did his hew deface. (IV.viii.14)

He informs his "dearest dred" that she is the worker of his smart; her "misdeeming" bred her displeasure and his dishonor (viii.17). Jonathan Goldberg suggests a connection between Belphoebe and Sclaunder on the basis of their misreadings (Goldberg 1981: 59–62,

152). He also implies a linkage between Elizabeth and the misregarding reader of the Sclaunder episode:

> The only person ever addressed as a reader [before IV.viii.29] is the "dearest dred" of the first proem; for instance, in the proem to book IV, she is asked to "reade this lesson often" (5.9). However, in the address to the reader in the middle of book IV, it is not even reading, but assumed misreading that is in question. Although, like the "dearest dred," this reader is being asked to read, the request is couched negatively – the narrator assumes that the reader has read and has (therefore) misread. (Goldberg 1981: 60)

Although Goldberg does not pursue the significance of this correlation I would argue it is one the poem deliberately establishes and sustains. By misinterpreting love as lust, Belphoebe condemns honorable behavior as dishonorable, and thus becomes a source and not a silencer of slander.

The Proem to Book IV attempts to juxtapose the misreading "rugged forhead . . . of state" with the right-reading "Queene of loue" both to establish a model of correct interpretation of the poem and to convince its royal reader that she embodies that model. However, the veiled critique of her response to the Ralegh–Throckmorton marriage precisely puts Elizabeth in the position of "ill iudge of loue" in the Proem. Sclaunder is also a "queane" – the sole figure in *The Faerie Queene* to be so termed – linking her homonymically with Elizabeth. However, Spenser here aligns Belphoebe's actions more closely with the misdeeming reader – since neither participates in slander out of spite – to avoid accusing Elizabeth of malicious defaming. His aim is to warn her away from harsh judgments of both his poem, and of loyal servants like Ralegh, without suggesting that these undeserved imputations are intentionally formulated. However, he cannot sustain this position in the subsequent books of the poem, where slander is no longer represented as misreading, but as a malicious, dangerous, and aggressive action, increasingly linked to the court.

Book V opens its exploration of justice with a return to the topos, raised in the Sclaunder episode, of a fallen contemporary world contrasted to an antique golden age. Elizabeth is addressed within the context of that time of perfect justice and the source of her power is represented as divine:

> That power [God] also doth to Princes lend,
> And makes them like himselfe in glorious sight,

To sit in his owne seate, his cause to end,
And rule his people right, as he doth recommend.

Dread Souerayne Goddesse . . . highest sit[s]
In seate of iudgment, in th'Almighties stead,
And with magnificke might and wondrous wit
Doest to thy people righteous doome aread. (V.Proem 10–11)

The praise moves into hyperbole with Elizabeth, styled as "Prince of peace" in Book IV, here again seeming to represent or perhaps replace God, by judging in his stead. Such high compliment serves paradoxically to dissociate the queen from the decayed current state of affairs over which, one logically assumes, she rules:

For that which all men then did vertue call,
Is now cald vice; and that which vice was hight,
Is now hight vertue, and so vs'd of all:
Right now is wrong, and wrong that was is right
As all things else in time are chaunged quight. (V.Proem 4)

This problem of defining and distinguishing right and wrong lies at the heart of slander whose operation inverts relations – the accusation is actually a false imputation, the defendant becomes the plaintiff and vice versa – in a battle for defining which language is "true." However, the poet can only attack vice by himself redefining good and evil and attributing them respectively to Elizabeth and her ministers; he can then condemn vice without directly implicating his ruler. However, a reading of the Blatant Beast's attack on Artegall within its historical context shows the difficulty Spenser has in avoiding this implication.

At the close of Book V, after freeing Irena from the clutches of Grantorto, Artegall begins restoring law and order to her kingdom:

His studie was true Iustice how to deale,
And day and night employ'd his busie paine
How to reforme that ragged common-weale . . . (V.xii.26)

To which end, he sends Talus out to discover perpetrators of both civil and criminal malfeasance, "On whome he did inflict most grieuous punishment" (xii.26). The historical allegory of this episode identifies Artegall, and in some sense Talus, with Arthur, Lord Grey; in this one line Spenser casts in quite reasonable terms the harsh policies his patron advocated and enacted as Lord Deputy of Ireland. However, in the cantos that follow, the poet acknowledges the censure – ill-founded in the poem's depiction – that Grey's tactics elicited by representing Artegall as attacked by Enuy, Detraction, and the Blatant Beast. Early critics who offered explanations of the historical import of the last canto of Book v allowed Spenser's account of Grey's recall from his Irish post to color their understanding of events surrounding that period. For example, Raymond Jenkins, who provides a fairly accurate account of Grey's tenure in Ireland, abandons his reliance on contemporary correspondence and state documents when he explains the poem's representation of Grey: "The Legend of Justice therefore became [Spenser's] vindication of his beloved leader, a just man who died in disgrace, undone by Envy and Detraction and the bellowings of the Blatant Beast" (Jenkins 1937: 353). In fact, Grey lived for more than a decade after his recall from Ireland, and, after an initial period of disfavor, pursued a moderately successful career until his death in 1593. Why then did Spenser defend Lord Grey (now dead) from a defamatory attack that was fifteen years old and appeared not to have occurred as the poet represented it? In order to answer this question, we must first take an extended look at events surrounding Grey's appointment to and revocation from Ireland.[9]

After years of unsuccessful attempts to subdue Ireland, Queen Elizabeth was herself apprehensive in the early 1580s of defamatory attacks with regard to her Irish policies, an anxiety that continued to make itself felt through the turn of the century as noted in the 1599 Star Chamber discussion of slanders, quoted in chapter 1. In her instructions to Lord Grey at the beginning of his deputyship (July 1580) she advocated a harsh course that would discourage rebellion but would not incur public dissent – a nearly impossible task. On the one hand, "he was warned to avoid the common fault of former governors, who had been too easy in granting pardons to notorious transgressors of the law, and had thereby bred boldness in subjects prone to offend . . . On the other hand the Queen was anxious to have it known that she did not wish to extirpate the inhabitants of Ireland, as it had been falsely and maliciously reported" (Bagwell 1890, III: 59).[10] Grey realized the futility of his task in Ireland less than a year after his appointment. In May 1581 he found himself facing outbreaks in the north, in the south, and in Munster; in addition, he was ill with a fever that had killed many of his soldiers and one of his sons. When he asked Elizabeth once again to send desperately needed supplies, she instead ordered a general pardon. "Disgusted with the Queen's inclination to let the 'Irish wallow in their own sensual government,' Grey began his pleas for recall" (Jenkins 1937: 345). While Elizabeth favored in theory a policy of harsh repression in Ireland, she was reluctant to pay for the expenses such a course would incur; leniency was an attractively inexpensive alternative to the sizable costs of increasing the militia. Grey's requests for recall continued until Elizabeth finally granted his revocation in August 1582.

While it is true that Grey was defamed in letters sent to the Queen during his tenure in Ireland, these attacks were certainly less the cause of recall than the Lord Deputy's own requests and the increasing disorder and violence in Ireland. Like all public officials performing an unpopular task, the Lord Deputy had enemies who sought to bring him into royal disfavor. Bagwell notes in his account of the recall that "In a letter to [Secretary Francis] Walsingham of July 2, 1582, Grey complains that Burghley listens to slanderers" (Bagwell 1890: 97, note 1). Nicholas Canny identifies the inhabitants of the Pale as the source of the defamations; when their allegiance to the crown was called into question after the second Desmond rebellion, the Old English saw their favored position in the governing of Ireland threatened.[11] Nicholas White, an Old English barrister who served as Master of the Rolls, was an enemy of Grey's and wrote to Burghley of his distress at the government of Ireland (Canny 1983: 13 14). He is quite likely the source of the defamation Grey complains about in his letter to Walsingham.

An examination of this letter of July 2 1582 will shed some light on the relation of the slanderous attacks on Grey to his revocation. The letter opens by responding to earlier letters in which Walsingham had discussed the prospects for the Lord Deputy's revocation.

> First, as tootchyng my revocatio[n], w^{c} a postscript of y^{r} last dated l^{t}r doothe, signifieng vntoo mee too stande now in waueuering, how euer certayne y^{r} oother & ye postilles of y^{r} collectio[n] doo make it, hath browght mee no small melancholie & in manner of dispayre of recoouerie.[12]

Grey pleads with Walsingham to let him at least return to England, if a thorough discharge cannot be obtained, so that he can attempt to work out policy disputes in person. Pursuing another tack, he assures

Walsingham that the situation in Ireland is not so volatile that it could not do without a governor for a month or two; Grey is apparently so anxious to leave that he is unwilling to wait for a replacement to be chosen. The two arguments the Lord Deputy offers contradict each other: the first asks to return so as to remedy his position as governor of Ireland, indicating his commitment to the task; the second suggests that his immediate recall would not endanger British control over the country. Both, however, show his eagerness to leave under almost any circumstances.

Grey's complaint of being defamed is expressed within the context of his larger concern to return to England. He refers in code to a certain person making accusations about Grey's finances, with which he did experience some difficulty and which would certainly not improve his standing in the eyes of the parsimonious queen or of Burghley, her Lord Treasurer.

> but I woonder not a lyttle at 10.['s] confidents [confidence?] auowtchyng so manyfest an vntrowthe, of my trowthe . . . well I perceaue malice, as well as kyndenes, wyll yet creepe where it maye not goe. Thowghe hee kyll my purse he shall make my lyeff neyther shorter nor heavyor, & fro[m] y[e] rest of hys spyght I nothyng dowght y[e] defence of my good God. That 324 [CSP, Ireland, identifies this as Burghley] is so heavy against mee I cannot settle any cause but onely 10.['s] procurement, for neuer any waye haue I dezerued amyss of hym, & heertofore diuersely I haue fownde y[t] I stoode mootche in hys lyking & fauoure; and now fynding y[e] chaundge, myne owane innocencie toowardes hym wylleth mee not to reguarde nor sorrow it; yet in trowthe for one thynge I stande in awe of it & and that is [a long code; CSP, Ireland, translates this as "his [i.e., my] revocation."] least hee shuld hynder it, w[ch] to p[re]vent & healp if it maye bee . . . I thought it not amysse too wryte vnto hy[m]. (PRO SP 63/94 4–5)

Grey fears the slanders spoken against him will *hinder*, rather than cause, his recall; his relationship with Burghley seems of sufficient length and strength that the Lord Deputy expresses no anxiety about it sustaining any lasting or serious damage. While I have not been able to find the letter Grey mentions sending to Burghley, or the Lord Treasurer's response, correspondence between the two of them several years after Grey's recall shows them to be on quite good terms.

So far, the defamation of Lord Grey seems to be the result of a struggle between English factions in Ireland that remained concealed from public notice. Elizabeth was apparently determined that this should remain the case. Bagwell explains that because "it was feared that a bad impression would be made in Ireland[,] Elizabeth . . . determined to send for [Grey] under the guise of a conference" (Bagwell 1890: 97). Grey did experience disfavor at court after his return from Ireland; this was to be expected given his unsuccessful and unhappy tenure during which he was unable to meet the queen's difficult demands (Egerton 1847: xx). However, none of the biographical information about Grey mentions a public scandal or defamation; the *Dictionary of National Biography* fails even to mention the fact that he was out of favor upon his return. Holinshed's *Chronicles* makes mention not only of Grey's return to England but of that public servant's popular estimation:

> The lord-deputy after long sute for his revocation received her Majesty's letters for the same, and in the end of August, 1582, after that he had served full two years, he delivered up the sword . . . and tooke shipping. The said lord Grey was a man of great nobilitie, and of as honourable and ancient descent, one that feareth God in true religion, and dutiful to her majesty in all obedience. And, albeit he had deserved well of that Irish nation, and had sowed the seeds of notable services, as well for his martial services as for his civill government; yet he reped (as his predecessors before him) but darnel and cockle. For they had among them not only conspired his death, for which some paid deerelie; but made alsoe sundrie complaints against him, to which he answered to his commendation and acquittall, and to their reproach for their ingratitude. (quoted in Egerton 1847: xix–xx)

Far from defaming him, these criticisms turn back against Grey's detractors to his own credit. Generally, this account accords with what we know about the accusations made against Grey as a result of the Old English–New English power struggle taking shape in Ireland in the early 1580s. Spenser could have been aware of some of the allegations made against his employer by the Old English, but Grey and not his secretary apparently wrote the coded letter to Walsingham. In sum, whatever defamatory attacks were made against Grey, they were confined to a relatively limited governmental scope.

An examination of V.xii.27ff will reveal how Spenser's representation of Grey's recall diverges from one historical record and in doing so points the reader to another, more personally significant, record of the author's concerns. Artegall's reform of Irena's realm is abruptly interrupted by a summons from the court, presumably from Gloriana herself:

But ere he could reforme it thoroughly,
He through occasion called was away,
To Faerie Court, that of necessity
His course of Iustice he was forst to stay,
And *Talus* to reuoke from the right way,
In which he was that Realme for to redresse.
But enuies cloud still dimmeth vertues ray.
So hauing freed *Irena* from distresse,
He tooke his leaue of her, there left in heauinesse. (v.xii.27)

Spenser omits any mention of Grey's desire to leave Ireland, and focuses instead on the unperfected state of reform at the time of the knight's recall.[13] By so doing, the poet insinuates the injustice of the summons; Artegall must desist from the "course of justice" he has wanted and has been ordered to pursue. The source of this command is Gloriana's court; "occasion" is blandly identified as the motive for suspending Artegall's quest. But this word does not necessarily have neutral connotations in *The Faerie Queene*. In II.iv.4ff Guyon meets Occasion, the mother of Furor, who is able to stir up his wrath by means of her speech:

And euer as she went, her tongue did walke
In foule reproch, and termes of vile despight,
Prouoking him by her outrageous talke . . . (II.iv.5)

Her speech is reminiscent of the "Menaces, Threatnings and other bitter words" Ferdinando Pulton identifies as leading to violence and disorder in the realm (Pulton 1609: B^r). The Knight of Temperance is able to vanquish Furor only by preventing his mother from communicating with him, either by words or by gestures.[14] Occasion presents a species of defamatory speech, similar to Ate's in Book IV, that results in angry violence. While the laconic "occasion" of v.xii may not contain the vehemence of the earlier allegory, its resonance with defamation is nevertheless reinforced by the suggestion that Artegall's recall is prompted by slander: "enuies cloud still dimmeth vertues ray."[15]

Spenser's oblique reference to the slanderous Occasion is sustained further in Book v by the appearance of the "two old ill fauor'd Hags," Enuy and Detraction. Just as "occasion" and "Faerie Court" are associated indirectly in stanza 27, the figures of slander in the following stanza appear to attack Artegall only once "he backe returned from that land, / And there arriu'd againe, whence forth he set" (xii.28). Ostensibly, these attacks appear to be directed against the state in the person of its loyal servant, Artegall. However, the defamations against the knight emanate from Gloriana's court, where his quest began, not from disgruntled administrators in Irena's country. Spenser transforms the origin and impact of the imputations against Grey to create an image of a dedicated public servant who, against his will, is forced by court slander to abandon his task.

The intimation that the state is engaged in detraction against one of its own officers is echoed in the self-destructive aspect of the allegory of Enuy. She is represented, as is often the case in allegorical depictions of envy, as gnawing on a venomous snake;[16] however, since Enuy produces a kind of thought-poison in her resentment of others, she actually feeds on herself. Spenser makes this aspect of the operation of envy clear:

> That euer she sees doen prays-worthily,
>
> . . .
>
> that makes her eat her gall.
> For when she wanted other thing to eat,
> She feeds on her owne maw vnnaturall,
> And of her owne foule entrayles makes her meat;
> Meat fit for such a monsters monsterous dyeat. (V.xii.31)

The representation of Detraction, harkening back to the problems of slanders fomented by the misregarding reader, Belphoebe, and thus indirectly Elizabeth, strengthens the suggestion that the state is working against its own best interests in repudiating its most dedicated public servants.

> For what soeuer good by any sayd,
> Or doen she heard, she would streightwayes inuent,
> How to depraue, or slanderously vpbrayd,
> Or to misconstrue of a mans intent,
> And turne to ill the thing, that well was ment. (V.xii.34)

Detraction also works by misreading or misdeeming, but the poem no longer offers the option of speaking words without intent. The "bitter rage and fell contention" that the Blatant Beast adds to the railings of Enuy and Detraction portray slander here as the malicious and deliberate misrepresentation to the public of a loyal servant's well-intended deeds.

The appearance of the Blatant Beast seems to preclude, both at the end of Book v and in Book vi, the more benign account of slander advanced earlier in Book iv. When the Ralegh–Throckmorton scandal is recast in Book vi, the effects of the infamy are more serious, violent, and enduring. In this retelling the elements of the story are dispersed and reorganized, but recognizable. Serena, "Ralegh's poetic name for his wife" (Bednarz 1983: 66 and note 37), replaces Amoret as Throckmorton and her defamation is represented separately from the attack on Timias. Nevertheless, the description of the assault on Serena clearly echoes the language of Amoret's capture by Lust:

> The faire *Serena* . . .
> Allur'd with myldnesse of the gentle wether,
> And pleasaunce of the place, the which was dight
> With diuers flowers distinct with rare delight,
> Wandred about the fields, as liking led
> Her wauering lust after her wandring sight,
> To make a garland to adorne her hed,
> Without suspect of ill or daungers hidden dred. (vi.iii.23)

While the language describing her actions – allured, wavering lust, wandering sight – sends up all kinds of allegorical danger signals, Serena's intent seems innocuous enough: to make a floral crown to wear. However, if this garland can be read as an analogy for a good reputation, that is, a crowning attribute, the passage suggests a great deal of circumspection is necessary to preserve and protect oneself from infamy. Serena's failing here is to be "without suspect of ill," leaving her unprepared for her attack:

> The Blatant Beast forth rushing vnaware,
> Caught her thus loosely wandring here and there. (vi.iii.24)

The virulence of defamation as represented by the Beast emphasizes the high level of vigilance necessary to protect one's actions from misrepresentation.[17]

The Beast's attack on Timias in Book vi occurs "After that [he] had againe recured / The fauour of *Belphoebe*" (vi.v.12) a strategy which insulates the queen from any association of violent maliciousness. However, Bednarz understands this defaming as an extension of the earlier one and associates Timias' assailants, Despetto, Decetto and Defetto, with the malicious slander of "Ralegh's unnamed rivals at court" (Bednarz 1983: 66). The combined attack of the Beast with human allegorical figures for defamation also recalls the joint effort against Artegall at the end of Book V.[18] While Artegall is bitten by the snake Enuy had herself been chewing and sustains a wound "that long the marke was to be reade" (V.xii.39), Timias is actually bitten by the Beast, and suffers intensely as a result. Timias and Serena are brought together in this version by the dangerous state of their wounds; he "likewise wounded was / Of that same Monster late, for lacke of heed," again emphasizing carelessness, not guilt, as the source of their scandal.

The Hermit advises the victims that they restrain their "outward sences" from exciting "fraile affection" in order to restrict the senses and contain talk "in due terms" (VI.vi.7). However, this treatment suggests that the victim bears at least partial responsibility for the assault, or that s/he in fact might in some way initiate the attack through inappropriate management of the affections.

> For from those outward sences ill affected
> The seede of all this euill first doth spring,
> Which at the first before it had infected,
> Mote easie be supprest with little thing:
> But being growen strong, it forth doth bring
> Sorrow, and anguish, and impatient paine
> In th'inner parts. (VI.vi.8)

The description of the Blatant Beast that the Hermit subsequently gives complicates his account of slander as self-inflicted. The Beast's attacks are represented as external, directed:

> Gainst all, both good and bad, both most and least,
> [He] poures his poysnous gall forth to infest
> The noblest wights with notable defame:
> Ne euer Knight, that bore so lofty creast,
> Ne euer Lady of so honest name,
> But he them spotted with reproch or secrete shame. (VI.vi.12)

We re-encounter the contradictory nature of scandal/slander which seems the result both of personal flaws and malicious imputations. The parentage of the detracting monster similarly suggests that its very nature is paradoxical. Its mother is Echidna, a monster the front part of whose body is shaped like a beautiful maiden, while the hind part takes the form of a dragon. She represents the hidden flaw that brings about scandal and is the source of self-inflicted defamation. Her partner in the creation of their offspring is Typhaon, "a great puissant wynde: a whirlwynde" (Spenser 1977: note to II.7–9, 661). He is the external component of slander that randomly bruits about false imputations.

The effects of slander are represented as much more grievous and resistant to redress in Book VI. Here defamatory attacks are analogous to, but more serious than, physical maiming:

No wound, which warlike hand of enemy
 Inflicts with dint of sword, so sore doth light,
 As doth the poysnous sting, which infamy
 Infixeth in the name of noble wight:

. . .

Such were the wounds, the which that *Blatant Beast*
 Made in the bodies of that Squire and Dame. (VI.vi.1–2)

While the wound is transferred in the above passages from the name to the body of its victim, it retains a metaphysical quality as well; slanders are not wounds that can be healed with medical treatment. The Hermit with whom Arthur leaves the victims of the Blatant Beast attempts initially to treat the injuries externally, but finds that they have developed into an internal infection:

quite they seem'd past helpe of surgery
 And rather needed to be disciplinde
 With holesome reede of sad sobriety,
 To rule the stubborne rage of passion blinde:
Giue salues to euery sore, but counsell to the minde. (VI.vi.5)

The mixed nature of defamation may actually be a reflection of the contingencies of the cure; if the external threat of detraction cannot be contained, one can only exercise self-control, making an offense out of a good defense. In the treatment of Serena and Timias the wounds recover something of the verbal nature of defamation as the Hermit administers a talking cure.

He to that point fit speaches gan to frame,
As he the art of words knew wondrous well,
And eke could doe, as well as say the same. (VI.vi.6)

As in Book IV, "the art of words," language akin to poetry, helps provide a cure for the effects of defamation.

Spenser's representation of poetry's efficacy in response to slander rests on his assumption that the former is rooted in virtue; in the "Letter to Ralegh" printed with the first edition of *The Faerie Queene* he writes that the poet's task is to instruct as well as entertain his reader.

> The generall end therefore of all the booke is to fashion a gentleman or noble person in vertuous and gentle discipline: Which for that I conceiued shoulde be most plausible and pleasing, being coloured with an historicall fiction . . . (Spenser 1977: 737)

The poem functions, at least on one level, as a type of courtesy manual; it is therefore not surprising to find that Calidore, the Knight of Courtesy, has filiations with poetry and operates as one of several figures for the poet in Book VI.[19] In the Proem to this book, Spenser calls on "Ye sacred imps, that on *Parnasso* dwell" (VI.Proem 2) to guide him to "the sacred noursery / Of vertue, which with you doth there remaine" (VI.Proem 3). Parnassus is traditionally associated with the home of Apollo, the god of poetry, and the Muses; here it is also identified as the wellhead of virtue. Courtesy, styled as one of the fairest flowers of virtue, is thus an offshoot in the genealogy of poetry.

In the first canto, "courtesy" is derived from "court":

> And well beseemeth that in Princes hall
> That vertue should be plentifully found,
> Which of all goodly manners is the ground
> And roote of ciuill conuersation. (VI.i.1)

This passage draws together virtue and fluency and prepares us for the figure of the ideal courtier, Calidore. The Knight of Courtesy's goodness and courtly decorum are enhanced by, and perhaps reliant upon, his facility with language; in him

> gentlenesse of spright
> And manners mylde were planted naturall;
> To which he adding comely guize withall,
> And gracious speach, did steale mens hearts away. (VI.i.2)

Calidore is a type of poet-knight who serves his ruler by promoting virtue and, as his quest to capture the Blatant Beast suggests, silencing slander.

The symbiotic nature of poetry and justice is represented in the meeting of the Knights of Justice and Courtesy. In associating Artegall, the representative of justice as well as the slandered Lord

Grey, with Calidore, Spenser also connects the silencing of state slanders with poetry. On learning of Artegall's deeds in performing his quest, the hero of Book VI responds, "where ye ended haue, now I begin" (VI.i.6); courtesy picks up where justice leaves off. Calidore's quest is to pursue and capture the Blatant Beast:

> the plague and scourge of wretched men:
> Whom with vile tongue and venomous intent
> He sore doth wound, and bite, and cruelly torment. (VI.i.8)

Artegall refrained from punishing the Blatant Beast at the end of Book V, although he demonstrates here that he did not recognize the threat for what it is – "What is that Blatant Beast?" (VI.i). Slander is apparently outside the jurisdiction of justice in Faerie Land. Only the poet-knight, whose medium is language, is equipped to handle the threat of defamation to the virtuous state.

However, as Artegall's treatment at the end of Book V suggests, the relation of the state to virtue is neither stable or clear-cut. The Proem to Book VI (cantos 5–7) raises the paradox, also addressed in Books IV and V, that virtue and decadence exist simultaneously at Elizabeth's court.

> But in the triall of true curtesie,
> Its now so farre from that, which then it was,
> That it indeed is nought but forgerie,
> Fashion'd to please the eies of them, that pas,
> Which see not perfect things but in a glas:
> Yet is that glasse so gay, that it can blynd
> The wisest sight, to thinke gold that is bras. (VI.Proem 5)

The antique times represent a paragon from which we have fallen away, but England's own Faerie Queene embodies that very paragon.

> But where shall I in all Antiquity
> So faire a patterne finde, where may be seene
> The goodly praise of Princely curtesie,
> As in your selfe, O soueraine Lady Queene,
> In whose pure minde, as in a mirrour sheene,
> It showes, and with her brightnesse doth inflame
> The eyes of all, where thereon fixed beene. (VI.Proem 6)

In fact, Elizabeth's courtliness exceeds "all Antiquity," but the use of the same metaphor of the mirror with which he criticized the imperfect contemporary practice of courtesy collapses the distinction between the two. Spenser's increasing inability to reconcile poetry and service to the state is a manifestation of the impossibility of both celebrating an idealized, virtuous state and correcting its flaws. In terms of slander, the poet increasingly finds that instead of protecting the state from some external threat of defamation, he is exposing the court as the source of defamation. By defining slander as specifically and consciously attacking virtue, and demonstrating poetry's origins in virtue, the logic of Spenser's argument must conclude that his attackers, including the state, are defamers. Conversely, the state is only virtuous to the extent that it follows the precepts of the poet.

Book VI charts a movement away from the court and registers Spenser's disillusionment with his poetic project; Calidore's difficulty in pursuing his own quest in Book VI is a manifestation of this same problem. Although Calidore's charge is to find and capture the Blatant Beast, he is clearly much more interested in the anti-court pastoral world. The speaker of the poem seems to chastise the knight for neglecting his quest:

> Who now does follow the foule *Blatant Beast*,
> Whilest Calidore does follow that faire Mayd,
> Vnmyndfull of his vow and high beheast,
> Which by the Faery Queene was on him layd,
> That he should neuer leaue, nor be delayd
> From chacing him, till he had it attchieued? (VI.X.I)

However, the explanations the poem offers for Calidore's abandoning his quest serve to justify this decision, rather than criticize it. Why pursue the Blatant Beast, when the court that the knight seeks to uphold consists of a similar engagement in slander? Calidore quite logically prefers to

> set his rest amongst the rustike sort,
> Rather then hunt still after shadowes vaine
> Of courtly fauour, fed with light report
> Of euery blaste, and sayling alwaies in the port. (VI.X.2)[20]

Success at court depends on rumor, which can as easily destroy a favorite as promote him. The speaker in canto x asserts that Calidore would not be "greatly blamed" (3) for preferring the country to the court, since in comparison the latter is but a "painted show / . . . as there is set for stales, / T'entrap vnwary fooles in their eternall bales" (VI.X.3). The poet himself seems carried away by his admiration for

Calidore's pastoral sojourn, and for Pastorella, momentarily forgetting his own quest in the service of his queen:

> For what hath all that goodly glorious gaze [of the court]
> Like to one sight, which *Calidore* did vew?
> The glaunce whereof their dimmed eies would daze,
> That neuer more they should endure the shew
> Of that sunne-shine, that makes them look askew.
> Ne ought in all that world of beauties rare,
> (Saue onely *Glorianaes* heauenly hew
> To which what can compare?) can it compare. (VI.x.4)

This passage is fraught with tension; "that goodly glorious gaze" seems alliteratively connected to Gloriana. Who else would be the "sunne-shine" of the court but the queen, yet it is this very light "that makes [courtiers] look askew." The speaker stops short of making Pastorella and the pastoral community the ne plus ultra of beauty and goodness by recalling Gloriana. However, she is recollected parenthetically and transcendently. Her "heavenly hew" suggests her sway is superlunary, ideal, perhaps verging on the inconsequential. Here the private pastoral world created by the poet becomes the locus of virtue that the courtly ideal failed to realize.[21]

Book VI opens with an attempt to protect the state, in the person of the Knight of Justice, from slander, but ends with Spenser obliquely accusing the state of slandering him. Calidore begins his quest to capture and contain slander on orders from Gloriana, suggesting that defamation poses a threat to the state; we discover later that the Beast "Ne Kesars spared . . . a whit, nor Kings" (VI.xii.28) when the knight ultimately (if reluctantly) completes his task near the end of the Legend of Courtesy. But though the idealized poet-knight of the antique world is able to overcome the Blatant Beast by means of his shield and sheer physical strength, the Elizabethan poet trying to serve the state in a more debauched age is not. The Beast has since escaped its bonds, reminiscent of the fate of Archimago/Satan who is chained at the end of Book I (xii.36); in echoing that earlier scene, Book VI seems to suggest that slander represents sin in general:

> So did he eeke long after this remaine,
> Vntill that, whether wicked fate so framed,
> Or fault of men, he broke his yron chaine,
> And got into the world at liberty againe. (VI.xii.38)

No one is now equipped to silence slander as it attacks victims in "each degree and state" (VI.xii.40). The poet, who in Calidore's time was the only one capable of quelling defamation, is now, by his very ability to challenge slander, most susceptible to the Beast's threat.

> He growen is so great and strong of late,
> Barking and biting all that him doe bate,
> Albe they worthy blame, or clear of crime:
> Ne spareth he most learned wits to rate,
> Ne spareth he the gentle Poets rime
> But rends without regard of person or of time. (VI.xii.40)

"Bate" is glossed by Hamilton as "bait: attack; beat back" though it also carries the sense of urging on; virtuous poets who challenge detraction are in turn attacked by it. The situation of "most" in line 7 allows it to modify "learned wits," but it can also be linked with "Ne spareth he most" to form a kind of double negative – learned wits and (if extended to the next line) "gentle Poets rime" are *least* spared by the Beast. The "Ne spareth" structure of stanza 40 is carried over into the next canto – "Ne may this homely verse" – to show that Spenser's own poetry is included in this particular attack:

> Ne may this homely verse, of many meanest,
> Hope to escape his venemous despite,
> More then my former writs, all were they clearest
> From blamefull blot, and free from all that wite,
> With which some wicked tongues did it backbite,
> And bring into a mighty Peres displeasure,
> That neuer so deserued to endite. (VI.xii.41)

Spenser shifts the blame here in a series of subtle movements: his poems are first slandered by the Beast; he then describes his detractors as "some wicked tongues," which suggests specific people; next, he claims these defamations brought him into official disfavor. However, line 7 suggests that the "mighty Pere" is the real target of the poet's accusation, since the verse never deserved to be indicted by such a figure; here the court becomes the locus of slanders against Spenser. The ambiguity of the syntax would also support the reading that the verse had been meant to accomplish better things than to indict a mighty peer of slander.

While Spenser has represented poetry as the antidote to slander and discredited his critics by labeling them slanderers, he is nevertheless unable to insulate himself from the effects of slander. The progressive flattening out of the allegory of *The Faerie Queene* in the latter half of the poem suggests Spenser's disillusionment with his project in the face of official disapproval. Angus Fletcher's discussion of allegory suggests why its basic structure might become problematic in a slanderous climate:[22]

> In the simplest terms, allegory says one thing and means another. It destroys the normal expectation that words "mean what they say." When we predicate quality *x* of person Y, Y really is what our predication says he is (or we assume so); but allegory would turn Y into something other (*allos*) than what the open and direct statement tells the reader. Pushed to an extreme, this ironic usage would subvert language itself. (Angus Fletcher 1964: 2)

The subversive quality of allegory makes it particularly susceptible to slanderous misinterpretation. The more directed and didactic allegory of Books IV and V, in comparison to the first half of the poem, appears concurrent with the poet voicing a concern about his work being slandered. In Book VI, the fear of slander is realized in the Beast's attack of the speaker of the poem. The verbal failure of his poetry – allegory is not understood – is linked with a moral failure in society – devoted public service is not rewarded. This in turn unravels Spenser's double aim of improving the state through virtuous poetic prophecy. The true poet works to silence slander for the virtuous state, but by the end of Book VI the state is increasingly seen as the source of slander. We can chart the movement of the representation of slander from unmotivated misreading to malicious attacks. Spenser offers the possibility of an unintentional or mistaken slander in Book IV; defamation of his poem by the state is posed as a misreading, which enables the poet to stop short of accusing Elizabeth of malicious detraction. However, with the Blatant Beast, Spenser figures defaming as malicious attacks emanating, ultimately, from the state; Artegall is defamed not in Ireland but in England.

Let us briefly turn our attention to the events of the mid-1590s, when Spenser chose to reshape the events of Grey's recall to provide an account of this shift in the representation of defamation. According to Josephine Bennett's account of Spenser's process of composing *The Faerie Queene*, the attack by Enuy, Detraction, and the Blatant Beast on Artegall was added to previously composed material relating to Irena in the winter of 1595–6, as the second edition of the poem was going to press (Bennett 1942: 191–205).[23] That Spenser was currently concerned with the slander of the former Lord Deputy is shown in *A View of the Present State of Ireland*, most of which he wrote, in all likelihood, during his stay in England in 1596 (Spenser 1934: 233–4).[24] In this treatise, Grey is described as "a most wyse Pylot" who guided the English government of Ireland through perilous times: "that he brought her saifelie out of all, so as longe after even by the space of xii or xiiitene yeres, shee roode at peace, through his onelie paines and excellent endurance. howeuer envye list to blatter against him" (Spenser 1934: 27). Although Grey was in Ireland for only two years, Spenser/Irenius claims that the twelve or thirteen years of relative peace that followed were due to the policies established by the Lord Deputy. This would go some way toward explaining why Spenser is so concerned in the mid-1590s with Grey's policies; he sees that the period governed by Grey's course of action (understood in the largest sense) is in danger of being discredited and discontinued. This is simultaneously a long-standing and a contemporary slander that Spenser feels he must fight off.[25]

Many critics have remarked on Spenser's political ambitions as represented in *The Faerie Queene*, but few have taken into consideration the specific political sphere in which Spenser was intimately involved: Ireland.[26] The closest the poet ever came to being a public servant was in the various minor positions and offices he held in Ireland; the position of minor landed gentry he obtained through the acquisition of lands forfeited by rebels would have been much less easily available to him in England (Norbrook 1984: 150).[27] The ultimate political stakes in Ireland, as Spenser saw them, were the same ones England faced throughout Europe: how to eradicate the Catholic threat? Spenser shared the radical Protestant military policy of Leicester, Sidney, Grey, Essex, and, to a certain extent, Ralegh, a group combining both poetic and political aspirations (Norbrook 1984: 131–2). Spenser's defense of Grey, like his poetic justification and/or support of Leicester, Sidney, and Ralegh, operates on one level as an argument on behalf of his patron; however, on another level, Spenser employs his political agenda in an attempt to reform England and advance his own position in the state.[28]

By the mid-1590s, Spenser felt that his chances for political advancement were diminishing with the worsening situation in

Ireland; it became equally apparent that his poetry was failing as a medium for political reform. He responded to the situation with a variety of strategies: the early 1590s saw the composition and/or publication of works that criticize the status quo and praise public servants (all in some sense patrons of Spenser) whose advice was often ignored by the queen: "The Ruins of Time," "Mother Hubberds Tale," "Colin Clouts Come Home Again," "Astrophel" and the defenses of Ralegh and Grey in *The Faerie Queene*. However, by the time we get to Book VI, we find the poet less and less committed to pursuing a virtuous political poetics. Calidore, the knightly poet of Courtesy, has increasing difficulty in pursuing the quest given to him by Gloriana. Political poetry is in some sense abandoned in favor of *A View*, his humanistic political treatise. In this work, Spenser attempts to justify a cruel and desperate scheme, patterned on the tactics of Lord Grey, that he believes will both glorify England and make his own career. The defamations alleged in *The Faerie Queene* against Lord Grey are actually the criticisms the poet himself expects to encounter in advocating a rigorously harsh policy against the Irish.

By representing himself as the victim of slander, Spenser extends the category of worthy public servants defamed by the state to include himself.[29] The Blatant Beast's attack on Grey at the end of Book V prefigures its subsequent assault on Spenser at the end of Book VI. By making the poet unable to quell slander, Spenser suggests that the court deserves the criticism/slander directed at it because of ill use of its loyal servants – that, in fact slander is brought upon the state by its own actions. The notion that the Blatant Beast is emanating from the state while attacking its own servants suggests a kind of self-slander, and thus recalls the characterization of slanderous attacks offered by the Hermit. There is something self-destructive in the state's defaming its loyal servants. If the source of slander is internal, the blame must also be found there. Spenser posits that the Beast is released either through "wicked fate" or "fault of men" (VI.xii.28); humans have perhaps brought about this plague by their own weaknesses.

Far from presenting official disapproval as a powerful, censoring authority for condoning or condemning poetry, Spenser locates virtue and hence legitimacy in the poet, the effect of which is to transform criticisms of poetry into illicit slanders. In this paradigm, the poet is not subject to state power, but, as the self-appointed definer of virtuous discourse, he exercises agency against official disapproval. Nevertheless, the poet himself cannot escape the self-incriminatory quality of the slander/scandal paradox. The instability of slander suggests that the victim may be culpable in his humiliation, and his charge of slander may be baseless; that is, a slander.[30] The concluding lines of Book VI suggest that the poet, like the other loyal servants represented in the poem, is thwarted by official attacks:

> Therefore do you my rimes keep better measure,
> And seek to please, that now is counted wisemens threasure.
>
> (VI.xii.41)

This statement is less a capitulation to the state than an ironic indictment of its short-sightedness in slandering poetic advice. However, the poet is similarly undone by the vacillations of slander. The idealized project of the poem to distinguish poetry from slander and advise and protect the virtuous state from slander cannot maintain the stable categories of virtue and malice necessary to sustain this vision. The sense of disappointment at the end of Book VI does not mark the victory of state censorship over a delegitimized poetry, but the inability of either ruler or poet to avoid implication in the workings of slander. Ultimately, slander eludes the stable categories of truth and falsehood established by both official and poetic rhetoric to contain it.

3 Satire and the arraignment of the *Poetaster*

In the 1596 *Faerie Queene*, Spenser attempts to champion the social and political benefits of a virtuous state poetics in the face of perceived defamatory attacks against poets and other public servants. By the turn of the century, Ben Jonson takes up a similar cause for satire, an even unlikelier genre. If Spenser felt that his poetry was misunderstood and misrepresented as defamation, Jonson had to face the fact that satire was judged to be explicitly slanderous and seditious; it had been outlawed by the High Commission, which had oversight of all printed materials, in 1599. In the years leading up to the ban, satire had grown to be an extremely popular genre that increasingly registered criticism of the status quo. As Richard McCabe notes, "Such pointed and articulate criticism in so popular a form must have given the authorities cause for concern, for there can be little doubt that the satires were being received by their readership as commentaries upon contemporary events . . . Everyone knew that real individuals were being attacked in the literary squabbles: why not then in the social satires also?" (McCabe 1981: 191–2). As dissatisfaction with Elizabeth's long reign increased towards the end of the century, the High Commission acted decisively to prohibit the potentially seditious and disruptive genre.[1]

Shortly after the Bishop's Ban, Jonson produced the first of three "comicall satires," *Every Man Out of His Humour*, which succeeded in translating the outlawed genre into a popular and licit dramatic form. O. J. Campbell notes that "[a]lmost immediately [after the Bishop's Ban,] authors associated with the proscribed movement devised a form of comedy which effectively preserved its salutary purposes . . . Ben Jonson's *Every Man Out* was apparently the first play consciously dedicated to that purpose" (Campbell 1970: 1). Joseph Loewenstein remarks that *Every Man Out* was a high point in what had been a particularly perilous and unprofitable year for Jonson: "its selection by the Office of the Revels for performance at court . . . argues considerable success. The Revels Office was approving the work of a playwright who had been jailed for sedition two years before his imprisonment for murder but was also a Catholic (and hence a potential enemy of the state), having converted during his recent imprisonment at Newgate. The success of the play must have suggested to Jonson the possibility of his own recovery from this perilous marginality" (Loewenstein 1984: 77). However, the play did not meet with unqualified success; Jonas Barish notes that Jonson was forced to rewrite "[t]he original ending of *Every Man Out* [which had] offended because it contained an impersonation of the queen" (Barish 1981: 137).[2] Nevertheless, that the play was requested at court despite its roots in the outlawed genre and its close brush with directly applying this medium to the queen's own person indicates that Jonson was able to bring satire on the stage with almost total impunity.

Jonson's strategy in this endeavor was to emphasize the positive and didactic function of satire. His identification of the new genre with the Vetus Comoedia in the induction to *Every Man Out* emphasizes the corrective aspect of comical satire. Scaliger's *Poetices*, referred to in *Timber, or Discoveries* and owned by Jonson, describes the role of the poet during the heyday of Old Comedy: "He could abuse individuals with impunity, on the ground that a deterrent fear of a bad reputation would reconcile men's minds to virtue and restore them to socially beneficent living" (quoted in Campbell 1970: 5–6). Jonson's notion of a *corrector morum* envisioned the poet as performing a social and civil function similar to the punishment of crimes executed by lawyers and judges.[3] "When Jonson dedicated *Every Man Out of His Humour*, with obvious confidence of their approval, to the Inns of Court," I would argue that he was "invoking a bond [not only] of common literary sympathies," but of complementary corrective functions (Herford and Simpson 1925–52, 1: 11–12).[4]

In the creation of dramatic, or spoken satire, the laws regarding slander were on Jonson's side more than he probably knew. Part of the ease with which he presented satire in the form of comedy was due to the opinion implicit in statute law that spoken defamation, while certainly capable of inflicting injury, was less dangerous than written defamation.[5] A verbal imputation was considered dangerous to the extent that it disrupted its immediate audience; while rumor was feared, spoken language was generally considered to have a unique and therefore limited impact.[6] Written allegations, on the other hand, could be disseminated, message intact, over greater distances and published or posted anonymously, allowing the defamer a potential immunity which could extend the maliciousness of his or her accusation.[7] Additionally, the Master of the Revels' supervision and control of plays, while occasionally posing problems for Jonson and several of his contemporary playwrights, was less stringent than the High Commission's regulation of printed material.[8]

In spite of the fact that he was able to perform his first two comical satires with relative impunity from official censure, Jonson anticipates attacks on the third in his Induction to *The Poetaster*. Jonson's strategy in anticipating criticism of his satirical comedy is multidirectional, as he fears assaults from both the state and from fellow poets. His principal response to skeptical state officials is to present satire in a positive light; however, this entails not only depicting the virtuous satirist as aiding the state, but also condemning the abusers of satire. The latter part of this plan engages the so-called "War of the Theaters"; this attack against poetasters' functions, as was *Cynthia's Revels*, was yet another response in an established argument between Jonson, Marston, and Dekker. In this chapter, I first discuss what I think to be the play's primary aim – the defense of satire against allegations of slander – and attend to the consequences the poets' quarrel had for this defense in my analysis of the "Apologetical Dialogue."

Jonson, like Spenser, reverses the accusation that his work is defamatory and counters that the slanderous misinterpretations of his enemies "make a libell, which he made a play" (*Epicoene*, second prologue 14).[9] Envy, the presenter of the Induction to *Poetaster*, is traditionally identified with slander: Spenser pairs the two (Envy and Detraction) in his representation of the disgracing of Lord Grey in *The Faerie Queene* v.xii. Here Envy's defamatory attack on the play operates not so much by misspeaking – making false imputations–as by *misreading* – misrepresenting the very words of the work itself:

> For I am risse here with a couetous hope,
> To blast your pleasures, and destroy your sports,
> With wrestings, comments, applications,

Spie-like suggestions, priuie whisperings,
And thousand such promooting sleights as these. (Induction 22–6)

One would suppose that this attack on the play, like the one described in the Induction to *Epicoene*, would be attributed to a misconstruing audience. However, the perversion of the true meaning of the play is here equated with destroying the audience's pleasure, suggesting that author and audience share a common interest. Envy's allies in her project of slanderous misinterpretation turn out to be Jonson's supposed colleagues, "players" and "poet-apes" (Induction 35):

Eyther of these would helpe me; they could wrest,
Peruert, and poyson all they heare, or see,
With senselesse glosses, and allusions.

. . .

forge, and then declame,
Traduce, corrupt, apply, enforme, suggest. (Induction 38–40, 53–4)

The "armed *Prologue*," who deals the final blow to an ultimately impotent Envy, nevertheless corroborates both her description of slander as misrepresentation and her identification of the author's slanderers as fellow writers:

know, 'tis a dangerous age:
Wherein, who writes, had need present his *Scenes*
Fortie-fold proofe against the coniuring meanes
Of base detractors, illiterate apes

. . .

that common spawne of ignorance,
Our frie of writers, [who] beslime his fame. (Prologue 6–9, 18–19)

The classification of Jonson's colleagues as the source of slander he fears most rests uneasily with his assertion that defamation is the action of the perceiver, not the creator, since his detractors are both authors and auditors. Is misreading responsible for the bad reputation poets, specifically satirists, have, or are satirists who slander each other themselves to blame? Jonson resolves this apparent paradox in the course of the play by showing that his "base detractors" (mis)-understand the purpose of satire to be defamation, and willfully pervert the genre into a weapon to attack the true practitioners of the art. By defending himself against attacks from colleagues, Jonson distances himself from and defines himself against scurrilous satirical practices. *Poetaster* is both a satire of the abuse of poetry, including satire, and a defense of poetry, especially satire, which when practiced correctly rids the state of slanders that threaten the status quo.

The first poet who must be protected from the onslaught of envious attack is Ovid, who opens the play by completing an elegy addressed to the antagonist of the Induction. In this poem he associates Envy with material considerations and conventional behavior, represented by the subsequent appearance of Ovid Senior, Asinius Lupus the tribune, and Pantilius Tucca, a dissolute, blustering soldier. Law is juxtaposed to literature both in the elegy –

> Enuie, why twitst thou me, my time's spent ill?
> And call'st my verse, fruits of an idle quill?
>
> . . .
>
> Or that I studie not the tedious lawes;
> And prostitute my voyce in euerie cause? (I.i.43–4, 47–8)

– and in the action onstage as Ovid chafes against following the lucrative legal career his father has chosen for him, preferring to forgo "mortall" considerations for "eternall fame" (I.i.49). Lupus and Tucca, who ostensibly represent "respectable" society, encourage the young poet to pursue law, but their debased representation of the profession suggests it requires little learning and fewer scruples:

> LVPV . . . a simple scholer, or none at all may be a lawyer.
>
> . . .
>
> TVCC And the lesse arte, the better: Besides, when it shall be in the power of thy cheu'rill conscience, to doe right, or wrong, at thy pleasure, my pretty ALCIBIADES. (I.ii.121, 130–2)

Conversely, in their attacks on players, Lupus and Tucca inadvertently champion the cause of poetry,[10] revealing themselves instead to be corrupt citizens whom the stage rightly exposes to ridicule:

> LVPV . . . [players] rob vs, vs that are magistrates, of our respect, bring vs vpon their stages, and make vs ridiculous to the plebeians; they will play you, or me, the wisest men they can come by still; me: only to bring vs in contempt with the vulgar, and make vs cheape.
>
> TVCC Th'art in the right . . . Your courtier cannot kisse his mistris slippers, in quiet, for 'hem: nor your white innocent gallant pawne his reuelling sute, to make his punke a supper. An honest decayed commander, cannot skelder, cheat, nor be seene in a bawdie house, but he shall be straight in one of their wormewood *comoedies*. They are growne licentious, the rogues; libertines, flat libertines. They forget they are i'the statute . . . (I.ii.40–53)

The reference to the statute identifying unlicensed players as rogues punishable by law strikes an Elizabethan note in this ostensibly Augustan setting, reminding the audience of the sometimes antagonistic relations between the current state and stage. The remark, because directed at Ovid, may also serve to recall that Marlowe's translations of Ovid's elegies – the version Jonson used for the "Enuie" elegy in Act I – were also under legal prohibition at the time of the play's composition.[11] The 1599 Bishop's Ban includes "marlowes Elegyes" in its list of books to be prohibited, controlled, or burned, although the *Amores* were apparently not among the books destroyed several days after the pronouncement was made.[12] Nevertheless, Jonson's inclusion of the banned poem in a play that took its form from a genre prohibited under the same interdiction suggests that in the face of legal sanctions, the playwright presents a defense of a variety of poetic genres in this play.[13]

However, Ovid's banishment in Act IV has led some critics to argue that Jonson condemns Ovid along with the poetasters; indeed, O. J. Campbell somewhat improbably holds Ovid responsible for the corruption of Crispinus and the social-climbing citizens.[14] Eugene Waith presents an account of Ovid's role which seems truer to the action of the play: while the love poet is initially portrayed sympathetically, especially in comparison with the poetasters and their scheming associates, he is ultimately shown to lack the true poet's ability to advise the ruler and serve the state (Waith 1951: 19).[15] Nevertheless, this does not explain why Jonson included a sympathetic portrayal of Ovid in the play at all, or invited comparison with his project of satiric comedy by assigning this character lines prohibited in the ban against satire. Even more ironic is the fact that the ban prohibiting the genre that Jonson champions in this new dramatic form lists two satires written by the master poetaster he takes to task in his play, John Marston, suggesting an even uneasier comparison.[16] Finally, if Jonson is in fact presenting a defense of poetry, why does he choose to do so in a play ostensibly devoted to condemning bad poetry and poets?

Jonson begins his defense by addressing the preconceived notions his audience may have about poetry and its effects. In opening the play with Envy poised to attack before the action has even begun, he anticipates that his work has already been unjustly slandered, judged as "nothing but *humours*, *reuells*, and *satyres*, that girde, and fart at the time" (III.iv.190–1). Because some have spitefully misrepresented poetry by labeling it lascivious or defamatory – common charges against verse in the early modern period – Jonson is obliged to meet and dispel these false assumptions. Only by understanding the abuse of poetry will audiences learn to recognize and understand its true form and function.[17]

The plight of Ovid in the play serves to address the criticism that poetry concerns itself with idle and amorous pastimes, failing to inspire or accomplish any worthwhile action. Although Jonson initially appears to support and defend the love poet, he, like Sidney, ultimately affirms rather than denies this reproach of love poetry. The playwright is careful to make distinctions here among and between the socially beneficial satirist, the relatively harmless, but ethically bankrupt, love poet, and the malicious slanderer. His aim is to separate true, and truly valuable poetry, from poets and poetasters who abuse the medium. Ovid is clearly less harmful to the image of poets than the detracting poetasters, but he nevertheless incurs the wrath of Augustus for abusing poetry and failing to teach virtue.[18] Ovid fails as a true poet because his concerns tend toward love and pleasure rather than didactic service to the empire; he cannot see any value in "the tedious lawes" (I.i. 47) which ultimately preserve a settled state. Although he does try to combine law and literature in a superficial way after his father's scolding, the attempt is half-hearted; instead of merging justice and verse in such a way as to produce virtuous poetry, the poet only succeeds at setting tedious minor points of law cases to doggerel: "*If thrice in field, a man vanquish his foe, / 'Tis after in his choice to serue, or no*" (I.iii.5–6). Even so, this meager effort to take the law seriously is overthrown when Tibullus brings Ovid a note from Julia:

> Hence *Law*, and welcome, *Muses*; though not rich,
> Yet you are pleasing: let's be reconcilde,
> And now made one. Hencefoorth, I promise faith,
> And all my serious houres to spend with you:
> With you, whose musicke striketh on my heart,
> And with bewitching tones steales forth my spirit,
> In IVLIAS name; faire IVLIA: IVLIAS loue
> Shall be a law, and that sweet law I'le studie,
> The law, and art of sacred IVLIAS loue:
> All other obiects will but abiects prooue. (I.iii.49–58)

Julia's love and the pleasure it can give become a law to live by, supplanting ethical and moral laws that the poet failed to understand properly.

Although Lupus unjustly accuses Ovid of seditious behavior, and Horace terms his actions merely "innocent mirth / And harmless pleasures, bred, of noble wit" (IV.vii.41–2), the young poet brings his harsh fate on himself through his blind devotion to love. By setting Julia up as his law and moral center, Ovid loses touch with objective virtue. He forfeits his exalted role as poet by failing to act virtuously, and thus opens up to even greater attacks the medium that has already been discredited by popular opinion. As the "armed *Prologue*" cautions,

> 'tis a dangerous age:
> Wherein, who writes, had need [be] . . .
> Fortie-fold proofe against the coniuring meanes
> Of base detractors (Prologue 6–9)

The best means of protection for a poet is to compose irreproachably virtuous works that provide a valuable social function, and to behave in accordance with these precepts. Ovid's banishment from court indicates the inadequacy of his works in comparison with the sanctioned epics and satires of men such as Virgil and Horace, whose virtuous example in both word and deed instruct the emperor himself.

While the poetasters of the play have a more debased and dangerous notion of the function of poetry, specifically satiric drama, they have a clearer sense than Ovid that satire and the law should work in tandem, rather than in opposition to each other. Although Lupus and Tucca condemn the stage for exposing their own faults, they have no qualms about using the slanderous potential of poetry and drama to charge Horace with sedition. The only flaw in their conception of state–stage cooperation is that their understanding of politics is as corrupt as their view of poetry. In fact, Horace makes it clear that corrupt, slanderous officials like Lupus are more dangerous to the state than the poet's "sedition" alleged by the tribune, or even the truly dissolute behavior of the poet-participants at Ovid's banquet. Horace vilifies men

> such as [Lupus],
> They are the moths, and scarabes of a state;
> The bane of empires; and the dregs of courts;
> Who (to endeare themselues to any'employment)

Care not, whose fame they blast; whose life they endanger:
And vnder a disguis'd, and cob-web masque
Of loue, vnto their soueraigne, vomit forth
Their owne prodigious malice; and pretending
To be the props, and columnes of his safety,
The guards vnto his person, and his peace,
Disturbe it most, with their false lapwing-cries. (IV.vii.43–53)

Jonson widens his attack on the abuse of satire to include the misuse of state power, both in punishing poets and in using slander to further illicit ends.

The perverted symbiosis of poetry and state authority presented in the plots of Lupus, Histrio, Tucca, Crispinus, and Demetrius has its idealized form in the alliance between Horace, Augustus, and Virgil in Act V of *Poetaster*. Jonson uses this positive coalition to address the popular misconception presented in the first act of the play that poetry and the law are in opposition to each other. His desire to create a satiric genre that is seen as supporting the state, rather than subverting it, is evidenced by the successive attempts in his satirical comedies to place the satirist at the center of political power. Robert Jones charts the movement of the satirist in the comical satires from an activist stance in the public world (*Every Man Out*), to a more elite function sanctioned by the state (*Cynthia's Revels*), culminating in Horace's status in *Poetaster* as Caesar's critical and candid advisor.

However, Jonson's attempts to distinguish satire from slander by moving the satirist into the court are more a defensive strategy than an indication of his political alignment with the ruler. Horace is allowed to criticize Caesar without fear of reprisal, and as a virtuous author (albeit of satire, which is a genre classically "inferior" to epic poetry– see III.v.16–24) he is associated with Virgil, whose wisdom and moral rectitude set him above even the emperor. The satirist seeks the ruler's approval only to the extent that it will authorize the poet's criticism while allowing him to remain free of state controls and perspectives. Jonson's own political circumstances were not as propitious for poets as his idealized representation of Augustus' court. Failing a ruler who not only authorized his ability to criticize, but also listened to his criticism, the poet had to rely on strategies of flattery which Horace himself can dispense with in the play (see III.v.33–5 and V.i.79–99). Jonson was not above methods such as *laudando praecipere*, praising in order to teach, to effect a change in official attitudes towards poetry. His aim is not to support state opinion, but to influence it, using the poet's higher moral viewpoint as a guideline. In the *Discoveries*, Jonson articulates his notion of the state as the symbiosis of power and poetry, ascribing to the ideal leader of a commonwealth the title and abilities of poet:

I could never thinke the study . . . of *State* [confined] to the *Politicke*. But that he which can faine a *Commonwealth* (which is the *Poet*) can govern it with *Counsels*, strengthen it with *Lawes*, correct it with *Judgements*, informe it with *Religion*, and *Morals*; is all these. Wee do not require in him meere *Elocution*; or an excellent faculty in verse; but the exact knowledge of all vertues, and their Contraries; with ability to render the one lov'd, the other hated, by his proper embattling them.[19]

Like Spenser, Jonson understands the poet's function as the curator and inculcator of virtue. In *Poetaster* he succeeds in imagining a commonwealth where poets act as virtuous ministers of state and the ruler sits at the feet of Virgil.

Horace succeeds at Augustus' court where Ovid fails because he understands that "meere *Elocution*" is not enough to secure promotion and influence at court; the satirist or successful court poet must appreciate that the virtue of true poetry is an essential and tempering quality in a successful regime. If Horace's enviable position at court gives him the luxury of suspending flattery when addressing the emperor, it also serves to present a prototype for ideal relations between the Elizabethan monarch and her poet. This model satirist is enviable precisely because he is free of feeling envy; having secured the support and esteem of the emperor, he need not worry about malicious attacks on his person or profession.

The groundwork for Horace's ultimate political triumph over and subordination of his enemies is established in III.v in a conversation with the prominent Roman lawyer, C. Trebatius Testa. This scene, which is based on the first satire of Horace's second book of satires, was added after the 1601 Quarto and the angry response which followed it as mentioned in the "Apologetical Dialogue." In this afterword, Polyposus reports to the Author that his critics "say you tax'd / The Law, and Lawyers" (81–2); the Author replies that he merely relied on biographical material from Ovid's experience with the law. Although this is not strictly true, since the worst things said about the law are not Ovid's complaints but Jonson's own fabrications put in the mouths of Lupus and Tucca, nevertheless his purpose in vilifying the law in Act I was to discredit the speakers, not the subject.[20] In the "Apologetical Dialogue," Jonson retreats from the typical satiric defense that only those guilty of crimes condemn raillery to offer what might be a sincere apology in the form of a denial:

> But how [Ovid's denunciation of the legal
> profession] should relate, vnto our lawes,
> Or their iust ministers, with least abuse,
> I reuerence both too much, to vnderstand! (Apol. Dial., ll.125–7)

The respect and gratitude Jonson had for the legal profession are indicated in the dedication of two of his satirical comedies to lawyers, *Every Man Out*, previously mentioned, and *Poetaster*. The latter was dedicated to Richard Martin of the Middle Temple (Herford and Simpson 1925–52, IX: 532), who apparently defended the playwright when the play first came under attack after its initial performances. It is possible that III.v was added later to reinforce his profession of respect for the law by depicting an eminent lawyer and satiric poet debating and then defending in tandem the value and function of satire.[21]

The original purpose of Horace's poem admirably suited the larger objective of Jonson's play: defending satire by demonstrating its affinity with the law. Herford and Simpson provide Arthur Palmer's account of the motivation behind the Latin version:

> This Satire forms a sort of general apologetic preface to the second book, and, though prefixed to that collection, was, perhaps, the last composed. Horace found that his Satire had made him unpopular . . . He had probably been advised to abandon it . . . and this poem may be regarded as an answer to those who advised him to do so. (Herford and Simpson 1925–52, IV: 194)

Horace's argument that satire cooperates with the functions of justice prevails against the reservations of the lawyer, just as Jonson hoped his play would alter the negative view of the genre held by contemporary officials. Although Trebatius finally begins to yield to Horace's reasoning, he nevertheless cautions the poet that the law might serve to punish satires:

> Better pause,
> Then rue thy ignorance of the sacred lawes;
> There's iustice, and great action may be su'd
> 'Gainst such, as wrong mens fames with verses lewd. (III.v.126–9)

But Horace counters that only lewd verses constituting libel of powerful personages are liable to such laws, and the satirist does not transgress these strictures (in language similar to that of the Author regarding the law in the "Apologetical Dialogue"): "I reuerence and adore that iust decree" (III.v.132). He in fact performs a quasi-legal function upheld by the courts themselves in attacking social crimes in the form of vice:

> sharp, yet modest rimes,
> That spare mens persons, and but taxe their crimes,
> Such, shall in open court, find currant passe;
> Were CAESAR iudge, and with the makers grace. (III.v.133–6)

Horace wins Trebatius over with this argument, suggesting the predominance of the poet over the law-giver and foreshadowing the action of Act V. The great Roman jurist insists on extending the satirist's licit power, thus sanctioning the behavior Horace is accused of at the beginning of this scene – "There are, to whom I seeme excessiue sower; / And past a *satyres* law, t'extend my power" (III.v.1–2). Trebatius allows that if the satirist is free of the crime he condemns, he is warranted in attacking perpetrators by name, predicting that if someone so exposed brought an action against the poet, "his [i.e., the person satirized] sute shall quickly bee / Dissolu'd in laughter, and thou thence sit free" (III.v.139 40).[22] Jonson encapsulates here the crux of his defense: the law is on the satirist's side.

In Act V he extends this argument to show that true satirists, far from being the detractors their critics allege, expose and silence their critic-slanderers who actually do threaten the safety of a settled state. The unfolding of the function of the true poet and his relation to the ruler with regard to slander begins in the inner sanctum of Caesar's court. The scene with Trebatius and Horace prefigures on a less exalted scale the affiliation between Virgil and Augustus, while also suggesting the correspondence between the two pairs: the satirist is necessary to the poetic support of state as is the epic poet, just as the jurist is indispensable to the political functioning of the state as is the emperor. Augustus is so enlightened as to understand the proper relation between poet and ruler. He equates Virgil with himself –

> Welcome to CAESAR, VIRGIL. CAESAR, and VIRGIL,
> Shall differ but in sound; to CAESAR, VIRGIL

(Of his expressed greatnesse) shall be made
A second sur-name, and to VIRGIL, CAESAR (V.ii.2–5)

– but rises in deference to greet the poet. Virgil is proffered a chair to the right and above Caesar's own throne, demonstrating his superior wisdom and ability to lead the emperor: "Vertue, without presumption, place may take / Aboue best Kings, whom onely she should make" (V.ii.26–7). Virgil, anticipating that this scene might require too great a suspension of belief for a early modern audience, registers the unlikelihood of this exchange, and suggests such actions cross the course of heaven. Caesar essentially equates the "course of heaven, and fate it selfe" with custom, insofar as he will ignore both where opinions of the worth of poets are concerned. He constructs a new cosmology based on reason, which recognizes virtue as the highest good. In this new order, the poet becomes the prophet whose vatic pronouncements will guide the course of the empire.

Tibullus alludes to the amazing applicability of Virgil's works to various circumstances in a conversation with Caesar:

TIBV That, which he hath writ,
Is with such iudgement, labour'd, and distill'd
Through all the needfull vses of our liues,
That could a man remember but his lines,
He should not touch at any serious point,
But he might breathe his spirit out of him.
CAES You meane, he might repeat part of his workes,
As fit for any conference, he can vse?
TIBV True, royall CAESAR. (V.i.118–26)

Jonson makes use of the popular belief in *sortes virgilianae*, a reliance on the presumed oracular powers of the *Aeneid*, to emphasize subtly the superiority of the poet's omniscience to the ruler's omnipotence.[23] Declining to read the text himself for fear of profaning it, Caesar selects a passage at random from the poem, as was the common practice, for the poet to recite: "and where first by chance / We here haue turn'd thy booke, doe thou first reade" (V.ii.46–7). The episode he chooses, the consummation of Dido and Aeneas' love and Fama's subsequent trumpeting of the event, establishes prophetic resonance and dramatic irony in its ramifications for the play's inferior poets. The fate of Dido and Aeneas, brought about by passion obscuring judgment, mirrors the doomed affair of Julia and Ovid, according to

Eugene Waith. "[In V.ii.69–73] Virgil is made to pronounce censure on the sort of love which has proved the undoing of Ovid and Julia, although they, like Dido, protest that it is virtuous love" (Waith 1951: 19). Because Dido is a ruler, such a lapse has catastrophic consequences for her realm: "*For now, nor rumours sound, / Nor nice respect of state mooves* DIDO *ought*" (V.ii.69–70). Julia, as the emperor's daughter, possesses imperial blood which entitles her, in the absence of other heirs, to rule. Caesar banishes Ovid for "soothing the declin'd affections / Of our base daughter" (IV.vi.54–5), that is, perverting and debasing a potential ruler of Rome.[24] The juxtaposition of these illicit liaisons implies that a ruler who fails to be guided by virtue, and, by extension, virtuous poetry, endangers her realm; the poet who actively promotes love to a ruler, or his daughter, over all considerations, poses a potential threat to the state. While Lupus' accusations of sedition were exaggerated and unwarranted, Caesar recognized a latent, though politically real, danger in Ovid's relations with his daughter.

If Virgil's text clarifies and condemns Ovid's predicament by viewing it through the lens of Dido's dilemma, it presages and identifies Lupus and his poetastical conspirators in the figure of Fama. This embodiment of rumor and detraction serves not only to introduce the entrance of Lupus and the co-slanderers, but also to predict their purpose to slander Horace:

VIRG. *As couetous shee is of tales, and lies,*
As prodigall of truth: this monster,

LVPV Come, follow me, assist me, second me: where's the Emperour? (V.ii.97–8, iii.1–2)

Whereas Lupus successfully prosecuted a case against the largely innocent, but fatally flawed Ovid, he is unable to implicate the virtuous, slander-proof Horace in his accusation of libel (Waith 1951: 19). Horace is attacked primarily for being a satirist. Lupus and Tucca alternatively refer to him as "*Satyre*," "*Poet* puckfist," and "*satyricall* varlet," and assume a manifest connection between satire and sedition. The tribune, alleging a plot against the Emperor's life, brings forth as evidence an emblem – "That's *greeke* for a libell" (V.iii.59) – which Horace has left unfinished. While defamation was usually conceived of in terms of the written or spoken word, pictures could be construed as libel, according to early modern English law. For example, the image of a gallows hung on someone's door would be grounds for an action on the case for slander, since a false accusation of felony constituted defamation.[25] Jonson opted to present a picture, open to misinterpretation because incomplete, as the basis of the accusation, rather than some written work of Horace's. The problem of ambiguity is thus connected with the unperfected state of the picture, and not at all with problems of interpreting the poet's language. In using a picture rather than a poem here, Jonson is able to lay the blame for satire's bad reputation on incompetent or malicious interpreters and avoids even the suggestion of equivocation or seditious intent in the language of satire. The spiteful reader/viewer and not the author is the source of slander.

Virgil's pronouncement on the dangers of interpretation as opposed to intent – of readers rather than satirists – is made in his super-imperial capacity. He retains his position of superiority during the questioning and sentencing of the conspiring tribune and player, seeming to remain above the fray.[26] However, his approval of Caesar's actions carries the full weight of both poetic virtue and state power, indicating that he, and not the emperor, is the ultimate authority. He sanctions the corporal punishments of Lupus and the conspiring player, but adds his own moral condemnation of their crimes in the form of a humiliating public rebuke:[27]

> 'Tis not the wholesome sharpe moralitie
> Or modest anger of a *satyricke* spirit,
> That hurts, or wounds the bodie of a state;
> But the sinister application
> Of the malicious, ignorant, and base
> Interpreter: who will distort, and straine
> The generall scope and purpose of an authour,
> To his particular, and priuate spleene. (v.iii.137–44)

Misinterpreters do not merely threaten state security, they actually inflict damage to the empire in misunderstanding and attacking satirists. In *Poetaster*'s attempt to realign early modern perceptions of the relations of poet to state along the lines of an idealized Augustan model, the ruler's enemy is not the satirist, but the satirist's critics.

The poetic justice of the play's action bears out Virgil's remarks.

Lupus is identified as a seditious libeler in his attempt to prove Horace one. The tribune's introduction of the emblem and his misapplication of its elements serve to indict his actions. The intended sense of the emblem is given by Horace in the following "*distich*":

> *Thus, oft, the base and rauenous multitude*
> *Suruiue, to share the spoiles of fortitude* (v.iii.79–80)

The image depicts a wolf and a vulture attacking an ass. Lupus immediately identifies himself with the wolf, thus revealing himself to be one of the base multitude who prey on the spoils of fortitude; Jonson presents Horace as forbearing and patient in this scene, relying on Virgil to speak aggressively in defense of the satirist. However, when Asinius Lupus also identifies himself with the ass, the animal immediately loses its "*hieroglyphick*" symbolism; Lupus is merely and obviously an ass. But in seeing himself as both the ass and the wolf eating it, Lupus becomes his own attacker, and provides a model for the self-destructive action of defamation. Lupus' imputation of sedition against Horace is transformed into an exposure of his own libelous plot.

While Jonson's main and culminating point in the play is to indict the poetaster, it is clear from his handling of Lupus that he considers the magistrate's threat to the respectable satirist to be the greater one. It is true that Histrio, the player who first informed the tribune of the libel, receives a harsher punishment – whipping – than Lupus. However, I would argue that this reflects the difference in status between the two perpetrators, and is not a register of the relative seriousness of their crimes. As a good magistrate, Lupus was obliged to investigate and quell false accusations, not exaggerate the situation to the extent that the accuser, rather than the accused, brings about a breach of the peace. Virgil's condemnation of Lupus is harsher than the judgment he later passes on the poetasters, indicating that the slanderous magistrate poses the greatest threat not only to virtuous poets, but also to state security.

Once Lupus is dispatched, Cornelius Gallus and Tibullus convince Caesar to authorize the indictment of Crispinus and Demetrius. The trial of the poetasters is the culmination of *Poetaster*, whose alternative title is *The Arraignment*. Caesar characterizes the exposure and punishment of the poetasters as a type of play, in which Virgil will preside as judge while he will "sit by, spectator of your sports / And thinke it no impeach of royaltie" (v.iii.163–4). The poets do, in effect, usurp Caesar's function by sitting in judgment of the accused. However, his willingness to allow them to do so implies that the poets and the ruler are of one mind in this matter, and that virtue will be equally served, or perhaps even better served, by allotting control over the proceedings to the poets.

As is often the case with plays within plays, this metatheatrical moment is a self-conscious comment on the function of the play "without." In *Poetaster*, Jonson arraigns the abusers of poetry while making the case to his royal spectator that she should allow true satire to be written and practiced, since it serves the very interests the queen herself wished to pursue. In portraying Horace and the other true poets as obtaining just convictions against poetasters, Jonson shows that poetry and law operate easily in conjunction with each other. However, he is careful to put the strongest condemnations of slanderers and, indeed, the very impetus of the trial in the mouths of poets other than Horace. The victim, though a professional censurer by trade, very modestly demurs when asked to arrest his detractors: "I am the worst accuser, vnder heaven" (v.iii.176).[28] Satire's overzealous accusations were as much a target of criticism as its defamatory nature; in fact, the striking similarity between a satiric attack and an official condemnation, a slander and a legitimate accusation, was a probable cause of concern for the state. While poets at the end of Elizabeth's reign insisted that their criticisms were in accord with the queen's own judgment, the state clearly felt, as evidenced by the 1599 ban of satire, that such attacks presented, if not a direct challenge to, at least an arrogation of royal authority.

Jonson dispels the notion of antipathy between satire and the law by portraying poets as maintaining justice through authorized legal procedures. The language of the indictment drawn up by the poets is modeled on bills presented against slanderers in the Star Chamber; Tibullus reads to Demetrius and Crispinus their indictment:

That you (not hauing the feare of PHOEBVS, *or his shafts, before your eyes) contrary to the peace of our liege lord,* AVGVSTVS CAESAR, *his crowne and dignitie, and against the forme of a* Statute, *in that case made, and prouided; haue most ignorantly, foolishly, and (more like your selues) maliciously, gone about to depraue, and calumniate the person and writings of* [Horace] . . . *and to that end haue mutally conspir'd, and plotted, at sundry times, as by seuerall meanes, and in sundry places . . . taxing him, falsly, of* selfe-loue, arrogancy, impudence, rayling, filching by translation &c. (V.iii.220–31)

In the case of *Elton* v. *Davies*, presented to Star Chamber in a bill of May 1606, William Davies is charged with a variety of crimes, one being that he, in collusion with others, defamed three people in a libellous poem:

by unlawfull confederacye aforesaid, thei the said William Davies and the said other lewd persons . . . yett unknowen, not havinge the feare of god before there eyes nor anie dutifull regard of your Majesties good and godlye lawes, statutes or ordinances have . . . seditiouslie contrived, made and written, published and spread abrode a most false, seditious and slaunderous and mallitious libell.[29]

Jonson deftly turns the legal language often used to indict satirical or slanderous verse into a defense of his virtuous satirist, Horace.

Jonson also counters the perceived opposition between poets and the state in Virgil's reassertion of the charge made in the Induction and Prologue: poetasters, and not audiences (including, perhaps, misunderstanding royal auditors), are satire's enemies.

And howsoeuer fooles, or ierking *pedants*
Players, or such like *buffon*, barking wits,
May with their beggerly, and barren trash,
Tickle base vulgar eares, in [the satirist's] despight;
This (like IOVES thunder) shall their pride controule,
"The honest *Satyre* hath the happiest soule." (V.iii.371–6)

Caesar's authorization of the conspirators' exposures and approval of the results bind the satirist and state together against both the abusers of power (Lupus) and the detractors of poetry. Jonson can thus simultaneously accuse corrupt officials of misinterpreting satire – a fault in the reader – and malicious poet-apes of misusing satire – a flaw in the author – without implicating either the royal auditor or her virtuous satirist.

If Jonson intends to align the true satirist with the good ruler, he also is eager to demonstrate the connection between corrupt officials and bad poets. One similarity binding Lupus and the poetasters is the self-indicting results of their attempts to accuse Horace falsely of slander. The poems in which Demetrius and Crispinus charge Horace with a variety of crimes related to and including defamation anatomize the poetasters' own crimes, as Virgil points out in his instructions to the jury:

> First, you must know
> That where there is a true, and perfect merit,
> There can bee no deiection; and the scorne
> Of humble basenesse, oftentimes, so workes
> In a high soule vpon the grosser spirit,
> That to his bleared, and offended sense,
> There seemes a hideous fault blaz'd in the obiect;
> When only the disease is in his eyes. (v.iii.347–54)

When the jury, which includes Tucca, returns with its verdict, the final conspirator joins his fellows in condemning himself. Both Mecoenas and Cornelius Gallus vote guilty, but before Tibullus can read the final vote, the captain interrupts him and changes it from the promised "not guilty" return to "Parcell-guiltie, I" (v.iii.419). This alteration is Tucca's attempt to hide the fact that he alone voted in favor of the defendants; he emends his decision to "partly guilty."[30] However, his words betray him into a confession of partial guilt, of having to share the guilt with his co-conspirators. Demetrius, realizing that the main instigator of the crime is allowing the poetasters to take the fall, seizes on the ambiguous meaning of the vote and uses it to expose the old "stinkard": "He meanes himself: for it was he indeed, / Suborn'd vs to the calumnie" (v.iii.420–1). While Jonson is concerned to punish poetasters in this play, he nevertheless emphasizes that the most harmful sedition comes from a state official, and that the poetasters are urged by Tucca, the corrupt soldier, to slander Horace.

All three of these conspirators receive as their punishments some form of public humiliation, akin to the exposure Jonson intends to effect by means of his play. Tucca is gagged and fitted with two masks, front and back, which declares his two-facedness and silences his equivocal tongue. Crispinus, whose offense against poetry consists in his disgusting language, is forced to vomit up his repulsive vocabulary in public and wear a robe, which would presumably indicate his crime. Demetrius receives the harshest sentence for being the most slanderous conspirator, the one most motivated by envy. He is sentenced to be branded on the forehead, a public sign that would last his lifetime, but his punishment is reduced, upon Horace's request, to the wearing of a fool's cap and coat (Herford and Simpson 1925–52, IV: 580–1, notes to lines 562 and 571).

Closing a play defending satire with a trial in which satirists are convicted and punished would seem a risky strategy. However, Jonson's purpose in this last act is to establish a series of distinctions that not only justifies satire, but authorizes it. He first establishes Virgil as the model poet whose epic not only secures the admiration of the Roman emperor, but also represents the type of poetry of which most early modern critics could approve.[31] As a revered and respected poet, Virgil acts as a powerful advocate for satire. He defends the discredited genre by arguing that the epic and satiric poet share the common goal of teaching virtue, albeit by different means. The roles these two poets play in the trial in Act V demonstrate their complementary functions: Virgil is the judge who demonstrates virtuous behavior so that others will imitate it; Horace, while also practicing virtue, enforces it by exposing criminals and denouncing crimes.

This symbiosis between epic and satiric poets may seem undercut by the divisions among the satiric poets themselves, but this perspective shifts once the role of the state is brought into the equation. The problem of slander is one that both the ruler and the poet have to face. Caesar must punish his subordinates within the government who promote slander instead of silencing it. Similarly, the virtuous poets in the play take it upon themselves to denounce poetasters who defame virtue instead of praising it. In spite of the similarities between state and poetic functions *vis-à-vis* defamation, Jonson does not wish simply to submit the evaluation of poetry's worth to a ruler's judgment. The Bishop's Ban of all satire suggests that the state would be incapable of making the distinctions that Jonson feels are so important. By segregating the corrective functions in the play – emperor punishes tribune, while poet punishes poetaster – the author maintains a degree of autonomy for the poet, showing him capable of policing the crimes of his colleagues and suggesting the state occupy itself with correcting corruption in its own ranks. However, by allowing Virgil and Horace to expose Lupus' plot, Jonson still reserves the rights of poets to identify and condemn official corruption.

Poetaster would appear to make a consistent and persuasive case against the slanders directed against satire at the end of the sixteenth century. By the play's end the virtuous poets demonstrate their ability to contain the threat of slander and punish its perpetrators. While the abuse of satire actually constitutes sedition to the state, especially in the hands of corrupt officials, true poets, including satirists, are able to identify and silence such dangerous imputations. The play also seems successfully to negotiate the Scylla and Charybdis of authorial intent and auditorial interpretation. By presenting the poetasters as detracting authors and Lupus as a malicious interpreter, Jonson accounts for the common identification of satire with slander without impugning the virtue of his own satirical writings or accusing the powerful members of his audience of inaccurate and unsophisticated interpretations. Jonson essentially agrees with the Bishop's Ban, insofar as he condemns the abuse of satire, and thus shows the state that it need not fear the correct practice of satire by true poets. However, he also advances the argument that true poets, and not the state, should have jurisdiction over identifying and exposing illegitimate and slanderous versifiers.

The play's aim of redefining satire includes reforming both the practice as well as the consumption of the medium. It would appear that the former goal – effected in the play by the castigation of the satirical poetasters – was partially successful in altering the debased style of a contemporary satirist. The emetic administered to Crispinus in Act v apparently had a real effect on Marston, the poet after whom this poetaster is assumed to be modeled, insofar as his characteristic "outlandish phrasing" abruptly disappeared from his writings after the appearance of *Poetaster* (Herford and Simpson 1925–52, xi: 578–9, note to lines 463–529). However, nature is usually not so cooperative in mirroring art. Caesar's speech at the play's close shows that he knows the value of true poetry and understands the distinction between poets and poetasters:

> It is the bane, and torment of our eares,
> To heare the discords of those iangling rimers,
> That, with their bad and scandalous practices,
> Bring all true arts, and learning in contempt. (v.iii.615–18)

But the events surrounding the "Apologetical Dialogue," as recorded in the addresses to the reader at the end of the Quarto and Folio editions, reveal that Elizabeth's ministers did not take an equally enlightened view of satirical comedy. According to the address in the

First Folio, the production of *Poetaster* was met by a flurry of responding "libells." Some of these imputations must have carried a semblance of truth, according to Josiah Penniman, because the author was apparently brought before the Lord Chief Justice "for his attack on lawyers and soldiers, and his innocence was answered for by his friend Mr. Richard Martin to whom he addressed the epistle prefixed to the folio edition of the play."[32] Jonson devised the "Apologetical Dialogue" to apologize for and to explain his play, but this addendum seemed only to add fuel to the fire. It was only once spoken on the stage, suggesting that it caused sufficient uproar to forbid its repetition. A measure of the volatility of feeling surrounding the epilogue is the fact that the author was "restrain'd . . . by Authoritie" from publishing it six months later in the 1601 Quarto. The failure of Jonson's play to redefine the official attitude toward satire lies not so much with malicious magistrates and spiteful colleagues as with the "Apologetical Dialogue" itself. The contradictory impulses in the epilogue and the tension created when these are juxtaposed with the body of the play show that inconsistencies in the author's attempts to define satire and distinguish it from slander ultimately undermine the strength of his defense.[33]

Let us first turn to the text of the "Dialogue" itself. The preliminary address to the reader sets out the issue that constitutes both the main purpose of the play and the main problem of the epilogue: how to distinguish the author from his critics, satire from slander? Jonson characterizes the apology as "*all the answere I euer gaue, to sundry impotent libells then cast out (and some yet remayning) against me, and this Play*" ("Reader's Address" ["RA"] 4–6). This account raises more questions about the "Dialogue" than it answers. If the libels were impotent, why did the playwright even dignify them with an answer, and why do the libels still remain fifteen years later? The author anticipates these objections, but in replying to them only manages to contradict himself: "Wherein I take no pleasure to reuiue the times, but that Posteritie may make a difference, betweene their manners that prouok'd me then, and mine that neglected them euer" ("RA" 6–9). In publishing his apology, Jonson does in effect answer his critics, giving up the moral high ground that he claims separates them.

Jonson seems to regain some of that ground in the opening

discussion of the "Apologetical Dialogue" ("AD") by demonstrating that he feels no anger at his attackers. But again he seems to undermine one of his claims with another. Nasutus and Polyposus find the Author musing on the response to slanders:

> The *Fates* haue not spun him the coursest thred
> That (free from knots of perturbation)
> Doth yet so liue, although but to himselfe,
> As he can safely scorne the tounges of slaues;
> And neglect *Fortune*, more than she can him.
> It is the happiest thing, this not to be
> Within the reach of malice; It prouides
> A man so well, to laugh of iniuries:
> And neuer sends him farder for his vengeance
> Then the vex'd bosome of his enemy. ("AD" 23–32)

The first half of this passage can be reconciled with the second if one takes the first line to mean that the Fates *have* spun a coarser thread for some, specifically the author, which enables him safely to scorn slanders. He gives proof of this in his claim to be beyond the reach of malice and his ability to laugh about his injuries. But the sense of the first five lines is more easily understood to say that the Fates have not yet spun a coarse enough thread for any man living safely to ignore slander or Fortune. This would set these lines against the meaning of those that follow, which makes a strong argument that people who are able to ignore slander know that defamation is its own punishment.

> It prouides
> A man so well, to laugh of iniuries:
> And neuer sends him farder for his vengeance
> Then the vex'd bosome of his enemy.
> I, now, but thinke, how poore their spight sets oft.
> Who, after all their waste of sulphurous tearmes,
> And burst-out thunder of their charged mouthes,
> Haue nothing left, but the vnsau'ry smoake
> Of their blacke vomit, to vpbrayd themselues:
> Whilst I, at whome they shot, sit here shot-free,
> And as vn-hurt of enuy, as vn-hit. ("AD" 29–39)

Despite the Author's claim to view the battle from the vantage of the "vn-hit," one can discern evidence of some shots finding the intended target. Although the author is laughing about his injuries, he admits that he is injured, and while he is beyond the reach of malice, he nevertheless seeks vengeance.

Jonson's concern in the "Apologetical Dialogue" is to maintain the distinction established in the play between his own authorized satirical practice and his enemies' illegitimate slanders. This difference threatened to dissolve when critics of *Poetaster* accused it of defaming others. The apology thus stresses the slanderous intention of these attacks against the play and attributes them to the very slanderers it exposed. The play's attackers do not aim to reprehend vice, argues the Author, since the crimes they allege were plagiarized, or only committed by the poetasters themselves.

> But . . . it is all excrement, they vent,
> Base filth, and offall: or thefts, notable
> As *Ocean* pyracies, or high-way stands:
> And not a crime there tax'd, but is their owne,
> Or what their owne foule thoughts suggested to them.
> And, that in all their heat of taxing others,
> Not one of them, but liues himselfe (if knowne)
> *Improbior satyram scribente cinaedo.* ("AD" 60–7)

He reiterates here the idea, presented earlier in lines 33–9 and dramatized in the fates of Lupus and the poetasters in the play, that slanderers, guiltier than those they are attempting to defame, will ultimately be punished by their own slanders.

The Author next defends the content and nature of the exposures he presented in *Poetaster*, contrasting them with his critics' slanderous attacks. He professes the play to be completely innocent and the attacks motivated solely by personal animus against him:

> Nor was there in it any circumstance,
> Which, in the setting downe, I could suspect
> Might be peruerted by an enemies tongue.
> Onely, it had the fault to be call'd mine.
> That was the crime. ("AD" 77–81)

However, the play opens with Envy poised to strike – by means of misrepresentation – and with the Prologue armed against such attacks, directly contradicting Jonson's assertion that he did not anticipate attempts to misinterpret his meaning. When Polyposus repeats the charge that the play "tax'd / The Law and Lawyers; Captaines; and the Players / By their particular names" ("AD" 81–3), the Author denies the charge, insisting that he spared persons and spoke only against the vices. Such charges of defamation are themselves "meere slanders . . . enforc'd by such / As haue no safer wayes to mens disgraces, / But their owne lyes, and losse of honesty" ("AD" 86–8); again, the attempts to discredit double back against the slanderer.

However, as he continues his defense, the Author reveals that the play was not an impersonal and detached satire of mores, but a response, albeit an allegedly unwilling one, to earlier attacks:

> three yeeres,
> They did prouoke me with their petulant stiles
> On euery stage: And I at last, vnwilling,
> But weary, I confesse, of so much trouble,
> Thought, I would try, if shame could winne vpon 'hem
> ("AD" 96–100)

And while he did not present actual names, neither did he clearly define the "crimes" he intended to expose; he charges his critics of being motivated by personal hatred alone, suggesting a feud rather than identifying a vice. Jonson clearly intended his satirized characters to represent actual foes and depicted them in such a way that they could be recognized by the audience.[34] Drummond reports in the *Conversations* that Jonson admitted as much with regard to Marston and *Poetaster*:

> he [i.e. Jonson] had many quarrells with Marston[,] beat him & took his Pistol from him[;] wrote his Poetaster on him[;] the beginning of y^{m} were that Marston represented him in the stage. (Herford and Simpson 1925–52, 1:140)

Not surprisingly, Jonson's attempt at embarrassing his enemies into silent submission backfired severely, eliciting instead an insectile riot of recriminations and imputations ("AD" 109–14).

In answering the specific charges of taxing the law, lawyers, captains, and the players by name, Jonson again contradicts himself in the justification of satirizing this last category. He admits to taxing players:

> And yet, but some; and those so sparingly,
> As all the rest might haue sate still, vnquestion'd,
> Had they but had the wit, or conscience,
> To thinke well of themselues. But, impotent they
> Thought each mans vice belong'd to their whole tribe:
> And much good doo't 'hem. ("AD" 142–7)

Instead of identifying a vice particular to players, the Author singles out a few malefactors and pardons the rest, turning his "crimes not persons" defense on its head. By claiming that most players took personally the satire meant for a specific few, Jonson also explodes the most basic defense of satire: only the guilty are angered by attacks.

The Author's deliberately phlegmatic response to his attackers is supposed to illustrate the rule to which he unwittingly takes exception in defending his own attacks: he is not angry because he is not guilty. However, as the mention of "injuries" and "vengeance" above suggests (29–31), he is not above responding angrily, even though "hypothetically"

> they that have incens'd me . . .
> know, I dare
> To spurne, or baffull 'hem; or squirt their eyes
> With inke, or vrine: or I could doe worse,
> Arm'd with ARCHILOCHVS fury, write *Iambicks*,[35]
> Should make the desperate lashers hang themselues.
> Rime 'hem to death, as they doe *Irish* rats
> In drumming tunes. Or, liuing, I could stampe
> Their foreheads with those deepe, and publike brands,
> That the whole company of *Barber-Surgeons*
> Should not take off, with all their art, and playsters.
> And these my prints should last, still to be read
> In their pale fronts. ("AD" 157–69)

The language of this passage conveys deep anger, even though the Author ultimately rejects such dire revenges as capital punishment by almost supernatural incantations and verbal stigmas reminiscent of the state practice of physical branding to which Jonson himself had been subjected.[36] He again asserts that such measures are unnecessary because slander contains its own punishment:

> This I could doe, and make them infamous.
> But, to what end? when their owne deedes haue mark'd 'hem,
> And, that I know, within his guilty brest
> Each slanderer beares a whip, that shall torment him,
> Worse, then a million of these temporall plagues. ("AD" 173–7)

However, the "Apologetical Dialogue" only succeeds in undermining the distinctions established in the play between Jonson and his enemies. In responding to his attackers, he acknowledges that he is guilty of their accusations and, by his own definition, if he is guilty they are merely satirists and not slanderers. Jonson's determination to differentiate himself from the slanderers he condemns, in an effort to distinguish himself in the eyes of the state, backfires on him. His depiction of the binary poles of virtuous poetry versus malicious slander leaves no room for the fallibility of the well-intentioned but mortal satirist. Even Horace satirized himself in his *Sermones*; in fact, the scene between Crispinus and Horace that works to ridicule the former in *Poetaster* is based on a Horatian satire in which the narrator as well as his tormentor are exposed in their follies. "As Horace's *Sermones* demonstrate," James Baumlin notes in a discussion of Elizabethan satire, "when the satirist engages himself dramatically in the world of his satire, his words and actions become as open to scrutiny as those of his *adversarius*" (Baumlin 1986: 460).[37] In Jonson's case, his attempt to exonerate himself in the "Apologetical Dialogue" from accusations of slander serves instead to make his actions indistinguishable from those of his enemies.

Within the play, Horace is represented as a satirist more sinned against than sinning. He is the intended victim of malicious slanders, but his own virtuousness protects him from the most vicious plots.[38] Jonson, however, by admitting in the "Apologetical Dialogue" that he is responding to provocation also reveals that he is responding to specific provocateurs, a fact he re-emphasizes in defending his attacks on "some" players. Here, he falls victim to the boomerang effect of slander he had attributed to his enemies. Like the poetasters, he also attacks persons and not merely crimes, thus making him a slanderer as well. Jonson's attacks against slanderers redound to his own discredit, and the distinction between satire and slander dissolves.

In *Poetaster* Jonson argues that satire, in attacking vice, avoids slandering individuals and assists the legal function of the state in punishing crime. However, the angry response the play received indicates that individuals did feel themselves to be attacked, and that some kind of disturbance ensued, bringing Jonson before the Lord Chief Justice. The Elizabethan state did not make nice distinctions between attacking persons as opposed to crimes. In fact, when verbal attacks resulted in a breach of the peace, the Star Chamber did not even distinguish between true and false accusations; criminal defamation was determined by its effects, not its content. Impersonation of actual people on the stage was also considered a scandalous libel because it was very likely to lead to public disorder. In admitting in the "Apologetical Dialogue" that he did write against particular people in *Poetaster*, Jonson creates the same problem for comical satire that verse satire experienced. In spite of his care in the play, Jonson does become his own worst "accuser" in revealing himself to be a libeler. The author's final attempt to convince official opinion of the virtues of satirical comedy only serves to confirm the notion that satire, in any form, was merely slander.

Jonson had no great expectation that *Poetaster* would reform his fellow satirists; he did hope that the representation of satire as he defined it might win the queen's approval and support. Ironically, while Marston showed evidence of being affected by the play, the state's view of satiric drama grew less accommodating, if anything. Ultimately, though, it is the logic of his argument rather than the power of state censorship that silences the poet. By insisting on the stability of what are inevitably reversible categories of just and illegitimate accusation, he falls prey to his own trap. While Jonson's slander circles back and "strikes [him] silent, seales [his] lips" ("AD" 216) against further forays into comical satire, he finds a new genre to suit his purposes. Tragedy, traditionally used to comment on the vices of princes, replaces comedy, which deals with the crimes of lesser mortals. The monarch, and not his colleagues, disappointed Jonson most in her response to the play; since he cannot find official favor with the queen, he contents himself with composing a play "worth the iuy, or the bayes, / And in this age can hope no other grace" ("AD" 235 6). The Author insulates himself "from the wolues black iaw, and the dull asses hoofe" ("AD" 239) – not from the poetaster, but from Asinius Lupus, the malicious, misreading, magistrate.

4 Slander for slander in *Measure for Measure*

Ultimately, Jonson and Spenser undermine the power of their critique of the state's assessment of poetry because their projects assume stable categories of right and wrong, virtuous and slanderous speech. As I demonstrate in chapter 1, slander is by nature unstable and draws its power from the inaccessibility of truth and the indeterminacy of language. Their projects collapse not because the state succeeds in censoring their complaints – the texts are still available for us to read – but because of the faulty logic of the representation of slander in state–poet relations. Ideally, both poets imagine an enlightened monarch who allows her- or himself to be guided and corrected by the superior wisdom and virtue of the poet. Both understand the threat of slander to a settled state and seek to protect the ruler from such attacks. But when they perceive themselves as under attack when their ultimately benighted rulers reject their advice and critique, they defend themselves by defining these attacks as slanders. Once they transform from advocates of to adversaries against the state, they open themselves up to the same charge of slander they themselves employ, and the match ends in a draw or worse, since they have insisted on the absolute evil of slander that they have now become guilty of speaking.

Shakespeare manages to escape from this conundrum by radically reconfiguring the terms of the debate.[1] As demonstrated earlier, the government was anxious to control for its own aims the theatre's power to criticize and expose; independent attempts to deploy this medium were distinguished as slanders. However, Shakespeare understands that this was not a battle between the state's truth and the theatre's slander, but a struggle to determine which institution would have control over dramatic defamation. The ability to humiliate, expose, and reprehend offenders – and thus to prevent others from offending – was claimed by both poets and the state. While drama that criticized the state or challenged the status quo was labeled slander and condemned, dramatic slander (in the form of theatre, court case, or punishment) that supported the ends of the state was condoned. Although the rhetoric of the authorities who attempted to control slander represents it as a threat to the peace of the realm, in fact the operation of slander constitutes in part (as we have seen) the state's own methods of punishment and maintaining dominion. This is the argument of *Measure for Measure*.

At the close of Act v, Duke Vincentio pardons all of his offending subjects with the exception of Lucio: "And yet here's one in place I cannot pardon" (v.i.497). He is punished, like Angelo and Claudio, ostensibly for fornication, and is forced to marry the prostitute who bore his child. However, when Lucio complains that "Marrying a punk, my lord, is pressing to death, / Whipping and hanging" (v.i.520–1), the Duke reveals in his reply that Lucio is being punished for an altogether different crime: "Slandering a prince deserves it." The Duke is clearly much more concerned about enforcing laws against criticism of the ruler than laws against fornication that he let slip, by his own admission, for fourteen years (I.iii.21).

Lucio is a slanderer, charging the ruler with licentiousness, drunkenness and stupidity (III.ii.115ff); similar imputations of a ruler's moral improbity brought several of Elizabeth's subjects to grief.[2] However, his accusations become relatively innocuous when compared to the slanders challenging the ruler's authority spoken, paradoxically enough, by the Duke himself in a public space in front of many of his subjects (v.i.314–20). Why is Vincentio so angered by the fabrications Lucio alleges in private when he himself publishes a direct critique of the state in full hearing of his subjects? The Duke condemns Lucio not so much for impugning his authority, but for competing with it. Lucio poses a threat to the state precisely because he usurps the Duke's ability to deploy slanders.

In order to understand the relationship between Lucio and Vincentio we need to know who the former is and what he represents. In the *dramatis personae* of the First Folio Lucio is listed as "a fantastique."[3] An examination of both the etymology of the term and its context in sixteenth-century literary theory suggests that fantasy is considered the source of poetic inspiration, and that a fantastic represents the figure of the poet. Furthermore, contemporary thought connects the fantastic with both a revealing function and with state policy.[4]

In his *Defense of the "Comedy" of Dante* (1587), Jacopo Mazzoni distinguishes between the intellective power that produces conceptions in conformity with the nature of objects, and the fantastic or imaginative power that is fitted to generate and create.[5]

Phantasy is the true power over poetic fables, since she alone is capable of those fictions which we of ourselves are able to feign and put together. From this of necessity it follows that poetry is made up of things feigned and imagined, because it is founded in phantasy. (Mazzoni 1940: 387)

Mazzoni believes that poetry is based on credibility rather than truth, and is therefore a sub-division of the sophistic. Recognizing that this characterization carries a negative connotation, he makes a defense of sophistry,

which, though it propounds to the intellect things that are feigned, yet does not disorder the will, but rather in every way . . . makes it comfortable with the just . . . And if it should appear to any one that it does merit blame because of disordering the intellect with falsity, I say that such an one should know that the ancient gentile philosophers . . . praise this disorder of the intellect in certain things, when it was directed to a proper end. For this reason Plato holds that the magistrate should be able to lie to his citizens for the sake of some public good . . . Now I say phantastic poetry regulated by proper laws is part of this ancient sophistic, since it also propounds feigned things to our intellect in order to regulate the appetite and many times contains beneath the husk of the fiction, the truth of many noble conceptions. (Mazzoni 1940: 369–70)

Mazzoni defends the fictional and fantastic elements of poetry by claiming that the state uses the same means to effect good ends. He even demonstrates how poetry was used by the ancients to regulate the different classes in society: the comic to make artificers laugh and forget their wretched state, the heroic to embolden soldiers and make them better warriors, and the tragic for the magistrates to keep them from being too ambitious and proud (Mazzoni 1940: 382–3). This argument suggests that the poet and the statesman work by the same means to achieve the better ordering of society.

In *The Arte of English Poesie* Puttenham also makes a strong argument for the symbiosis of poetry and government by referring to historical precedent. In former ages, good poets

were highly esteemed and much fauored of the greatest princes . . . [N]or this reputation was giuen them in ancient times altogether in respect that

Poesie was a delicate arte, and the poets themselues cunning Prince-pleasers, but for that also they were thought for their vniuersal knowledge to be very sufficient men for the greatest charges in their common wealthes, were it for counsell or for conduct, whereby no man need to doubt but that both skills may very well concurre and be most excellent in one person. (Puttenham 1936: 16–17)

In the course of this discussion Puttenham lists several rulers who were poets, including Julius Caesar, and other poets who were considered capable of governing, such as Horace. However, the poets of Puttenham's England no longer enjoy this esteem. Like Mazzoni, his contemporaries connect the fantastical with poetry, but with a less flattering comparison:

For as well Poets as Poesie are despised . . . [and] who so is studious in th'Arte or shewes him selfe excellent in it, they call him in disdayne a *phantasticall*: and a light headed or phantasticall man (by conuersion) they call a Poet. (Puttenham 1936: 18)

In the passage that follows, Puttenham explains that the fantastic is commonly misunderstood. He likens it to a mirror: "[t]here be . . . glasses that shew thinges exceedingly faire and comely, others that shew figures very monstrous & illfauored." If the fantasy is disordered it can hinder the sound judgment and discourse of the brain; "but when it is well affected it is of such great assistance to the inuentive part of the mind"

as without it no man could deuise any new or rare thing: and where it is not excellent in his kind, there could be no politique Captaine, nor any witty enginer or conning artificer, nor yet any law maker or counsellor of deepe discourse. (Puttenham 1936: 19)

Those persons whose imaginations are in disarray are known as a "*phantastici*," but

such persons as be illuminated with the brightest irradiations of knowledge . . . are called . . . *euphantasiote*, and of this sorte of phantasie are all good Poets . . . all Legislators Polititiens & Counsellours of estate, in whose exercises the inuentive part is most employed and is to the sound & true iudgement of man most needful. (Puttenham 1936: 19–20)

Thus Puttenham links what is good in the fantastic poet with the minister of state in an effort to demonstrate that the former provides the same valuable function for society.

Another aspect of the fantastic that would have been available to

Shakespeare and his contemporaries derives from the etymology of the word. According to the *OED*, "fantasy" finds its root in the Greek *phantasia*, "a making visible," and *phanein*, "to show." The fantastic could therefore be understood both as the "faculty of sensuous perception [and] of imagination." In other words, it could reveal the truth as well as create an illusion – like Mazzoni's suggestion that the fantastic "many times contains beneath the husk of the fiction, the truth of many noble conceptions" (Mazzoni 1940: 370). However, as suggested earlier, the capacity for exposure expressed in *phanein* seems to share an etymological root with *phanai*, that is, with speaking, fame, and defaming.

In fact, the fantastic's revealing function is very similar to the way in which dramatic defamation gives voice to embarrassing claims about a person. In the first act of *Measure for Measure*, Lucio displays how his creative wit discloses the flaws of his companions. In a conversation with two gentlemen, he notes and illustrates the hypocrisy of one in the tale of the sanctimonious pirate. When the first gentleman attempts to defend himself, Lucio turns the latter's retorts into a self-incrimination:

1 GENT: . . . I had as lief be a list of an English kersey, as be piled, as thou art piled, for a French velvet. Do I speak feelingly now?
LUCIO: I think thou dost: and indeed, with most painful feeling of thy speech. I will, out of thine own confession, learn to begin thy health; but whilst I live, forget to drink after thee.
1 GENT: I think I have done myself wrong, have I not?
2 GENT: Yes, that thou hast, whether thou art tainted or free. (I.ii.31–40)

Lucio deftly deflects and reflects this attempt to slander him back on the speaker. Like the mirror in Puttenham's discussion of the fantastic, he shows the attacker his own faults rather than allowing him to focus on Lucio's. His very name suggests his ability to reflect what surrounds him; *luce* means "light," as well as "looking glass," and it can also signify the capacity of discernment, artistic perfection, and fame (*Grande Dizionario della Lingua Italiana* 1975).

Lucio's conversation with Isabella in the convent retains the wittiness of his earlier language ("Hail virgin, if you be" [I.iv.16]), but, attending to the decorum of his surroundings, he addresses her in blank verse which expresses both moral restraint and ornamental formality.

> I would not, though 'tis my familiar sin,
> With maids to seem the lapwing, and to jest
> Tongue far from heart, play with all virgins so.
> I hold you as a thing enskied and sainted
> By your renouncement, an immortal spirit,
> And to be talk'd with in sincerity,
> As with a saint. (I.iv.31–7)

His language reveals something about Isabella's character that, judging from her response, she is uncomfortable about acknowledging: "You do blaspheme the good, in mocking me" (39). However, Lucio's solicitousness for her piousness and chastity foreshadows Isabella's own behavior later on in the play.

Lucio's ability to reflect and reveal something about the other characters has a dramaturgical aspect as well.[6] When Isabella's first plea to Angelo is met with refusal, she accepts his answer and turns to leave. Lucio convinces her to stay, and proceeds to block her movements and supply her lines in an effort to improve her performance:

> Give't not o'er so. – To him again, entreat him,
> Kneel down before him, hang upon his gown;
> You are too cold. If you should need a pin,
> You could not with more tame tongue desire it.
> To him, I say. (II.ii.43–7)

He continues to coach Isabella throughout the rest of her audience with Angelo, providing encouragement and advice: "Ay touch him: there's the vein" (70); "Art avis'd o'that? More on't" (133). Finally, at the appropriate moment, he gives her the cue to exit: "Go to; 'tis well: away!" (157). Lucio's staging of Isabella's request is disastrously successful, placing her in an impossible dilemma. However, her passionate plea does strike a chord in Angelo which forces him, at least ostensibly, to capitulate to her request. If his promise is not finally kept, it is not because Isabella's importuning is a failure. Rather, it is a tribute to Lucio's talents that she is able to move the deputy as much as she does; Angelo had every intention of refusing all requests to pardon Claudio, even Escalus' (II.i.1–31), and Isabella was convinced she would fail even before she met the deputy (I.iv.75–6, 77). Most important here is that Lucio's fantastical direction discloses an aspect of Angelo's character with which the deputy himself had never come to terms.

However, Lucio's most effective performance as a fantastic occurs in his remarks concerning, or scenes with, the Duke, about whom he appears to know quite a lot. At the opening of I.ii, Lucio demonstrates that he is apprised of the latest gossip on the Duke's mission, but in his discussion with Isabella later in the act, he indicates that he is not taken in by the rumors:

> The Duke is very strangely gone from hence;
> Bore many gentlemen – myself being one –
> In hand, and hope of action: but we do learn,
> By those that know the very nerves of state,
> His giving out were of an infinite distance
> From his true-meant design. (I.iv.50–5)

It is impossible to know if Lucio does have contacts in the government or whether he simply fabricates this explanation. What is significant about this statement is that it provides a remarkably accurate account of the Duke's plans. Lucio continues to express his fantastical insights in his conversation with the disguised Duke in III.ii. Several critics have noted that Lucio's speculations are uncanny in their accuracy.[7] Vincentio, disguised as a friar or mendicant, is figuratively "in Rome" (92), and does in fact "usurp the beggary he was never born to" (96–7). Lucio's fantastical descriptions of Angelo's "creation" do contain a grain of truth in them (III.ii.99–108); in fact, his remarks parallel comments the Duke has made to Friar Thomas about the deputy's preciseness (I.iii.50–4).

Although the account of Angelo strikes the disguised Duke as funny (III.ii.109), it marks the point at which Lucio's fictions become slanders.[8] While Vincentio ignores this criticism of his deputy, he lashes out when Lucio shifts his attention to the absent Duke. Lucio's first fantastical slander of the Duke portrays him as lascivious: "He had some feeling of the sport; he knew the service; and that instructed him to mercy" (III.ii.115–16). The suggestion that the Duke is promiscuous seems blatantly untrue; after all, he tells Friar Thomas in I.ii that the "dribbling dart of love" never pierced his "complete bosom" (2–3), and later in III.ii, disguised as a friar, he condemns with vehement disgust the act Pompey's occupation promotes:

> Do thou but think
> What 'tis to cram a maw or clothe a back
> From such a filthy vice. Say to thyself,

> From their abominable and beastly touches
> I drink, I eat, array myself, and live. (20–4)

Yet the Duke freely admits that he is responsible for the present licentiousness of Vienna ("'twas my fault to give the people scope" [I.iii.35]), and is unwilling to rectify the problem himself – thus the necessity for appointing Angelo. By the play's end the lapse still has not been redressed; Vincentio pardons rather than punishes the fornicators. Lucio's witticisms here pinpoint what seems to be a significant inadequacy in the Duke's actions as a ruler.[9]

The two pronouncements on the Duke's character that follow, that he is "A very superficial, ignorant, unweighing fellow" (III.ii.130), and that he "would have dark deeds darkly answered" (III.ii.171), also contain elements of truth. If Angelo was appointed in order to enforce the fornication law, the Duke could scarcely have selected a more disastrous candidate; his decision appears distinctly ill-considered, especially with as qualified a candidate as Escalus at hand. That Vincentio would answer "dark deeds darkly" also seems borne out by the fact that he prefers an indirect method of alleviating Vienna's troubles, both in authorizing a deputy to solve its problems and in his own behind-the-scenes manipulation of the situation. Again, these apparently fictitious remarks contain truths that call into question the Duke's ability to rule, and, if published, theoretically could constitute seditious slander. However, Lucio's most astute insight about the Duke is that the latter is a fantastic too (see III.ii.89 and IV.iii.156). An examination of the Duke's actions shows them to be almost identical to Lucio's, with one difference. If Lucio's fictions have had the limited effect of revealing the flaws in other characters' personalities, the Duke's elaborate plans constitute a full-scale exposure of Viennese society.

The play opens with a mutual address between the Duke and Escalus – Duke: "Escalus," Escalus: "My lord" – which suggests a mirroring or even a potential equation of the two public officials. The effect of the speech that follows reinforces this sense of Escalus' knowledge of statecraft being equal to Vincentio's. However, immediately following the establishment of this parallel, the Duke announces his imminent departure and appoints Angelo as his deputy: "At our remove, be thou at full ourself" (I.i.43). The choice seems oddly inappropriate; why should Escalus, who is "first in question," be Angelo's "secondary" (I.i.46)? As we discover in I.iii, this appointment and the Duke's hasty departure are part of a strategy of fictions he plans to deploy. Vincentio claims that his self-imposed absence from the ducal seat is a way of bringing his subjects back into a closer observance of the statutes prohibiting fornication. Because it would appear too tyrannous to enforce laws that he let "slip," he has appointed Angelo as his substitute:

> Who may in th'ambush of my name strike home,
> And yet my nature never in the fight
> To do in slander. (I.iii.41–3)

Although the Duke expresses disapproval of and disgust for illicit sex in his scenes with Juliet and Pompey (II.ii and III.ii), his scheme to couple Mariana and Angelo indicates that he is not above making use of it to further his own ends. His main motive for selecting a deputy is not so much to rectify the law but to protect his reputation; his anxiety about public opinion is made clear by its reiteration throughout his later speeches.

But the Duke offers another motive for choosing Angelo. Vincentio professes to know Angelo's real worth and ability:

> There is a kind of character in thy life
> That to th'observer doth thy history
> Fully unfold . . . (I.i.27–9)

However, he suggests to Friar Thomas that the deputy's character might not jibe with his history:

> Lord Angelo is precise;
> Stands at guard with Envy; scarce confesses
> That his blood flows; or that his appetite
> Is more to bread than stone. Hence shall we see
> If power change purpose, what our seemers be. (I.i.50–4)

In fact, the Duke already does know from Angelo's history that he has been less than just in his dealings with Mariana. While the Duke is careful to keep his own reputation from exposure ("I love the people, / But do not like to stage me to their eyes" [I.i.67–8]; "I have ever lov'd the life remov'd" [I.iii.8]), he is very eager to discover if Angelo's reputation is all it seems to be. The Duke's decision to spy on Angelo in the guise of a friar suggests a strategic fiction which will put to the test – and possibly debunk – the substitute's apparent virtuousness.

Vincentio's suspicions about his deputy are confirmed when he overhears Isabella's disclosure of Angelo's terms for her brother's pardon. The disguised Duke, who moments earlier while shriving Claudio did not indicate he felt the sentence was unjust, begins constructing an elaborate plan to save the prisoner and expose Angelo. When he asks Isabella what she plans to do she replies: "If ever [the Duke] return, and I can speak with him, I will open my lips in vain or discover his government" (III.i.191–3). The novice's accusation of Angelo would seem to spill over into a complaint of the Duke's own government. The Friar-Duke suggests a strategy which will effectively focus the blame entirely on the deputy. Because Angelo has only propositioned Isabella, he can avoid the accusation; the Duke devises a plan which will allow his substitute to incriminate himself fully and provide Vincentio with the opportunity to expose the crime, while protecting himself from blame.

In conversations with Isabella (III.ii.257ff) and Mariana (IV.i.71ff) the Duke justifies the use of deception by demonstrating the benefits the scheme will effect. However, while he plans to save Isabella's brother and provide restitution for Mariana, Vincentio's primary aim is to humiliate Angelo. Once he proposes the plan to Isabella, the disguised Duke starts setting the stage, as it were, for Angelo's exposure by making several apparently offhand remarks to a variety of characters. When Elbow mentions that he must take Pompey before Angelo, the Friar-Duke replies: "That we were all, as some would seem to be, / From our faults, as faults from seeming, free!" (III.ii.37–8). At the end of this scene, in a discussion in which Escalus mentions Angelo's severity, the Duke responds:

> If his own life answer the straitness of his
> proceeding, it shall become him well: wherein
> if he chance to fail, he hath sentenced himself. (III.ii.249–51)

In IV.ii, when the Provost displays momentary anger at Angelo's "bitterness," the Friar-Duke chides him:

> Not so, not so; his life is parallel'd
> Even with the stroke and line of his great justice.
> He doth with holy abstinence subdue
> That in himself which he spurs on his power
> To qualify in others: were he meal'd with that
> Which he corrects, then were he tyrannous;
> But this being so, he's just. (77–83)

The effect of these comments is to heighten the tension and resentment that already exist around Angelo so that his final exposure will be all the more mortifying.

Further evidence of the Duke's attempts to expose and slander Angelo, instead of simply rectifying the situation, is his manipulation of Isabella. Although Vincentio finds a way to preserve Claudio's life when Angelo refuses to grant the promised pardon, the disguised Duke informs Isabella only that the deputy has ordered her brother's execution. Predictably enough, Isabella is infuriated by Angelo's treachery, and again the Duke shapes her anger to suit his purposes. He dissuades her from confronting the deputy immediately, counseling her instead to accuse Angelo in front of an audience:

> you shall have your bosom on this wretch,
> Grace of the Duke, revenges to your heart,
> And general honour.
> . . .
> [T]o the head of Angelo
> Accuse him home and home. (IV.iii.134–6, 142–3)

Vincentio then insures that a number of witnesses will observe this accusation by sending letters to Angelo and his friends, instructing the former to proclaim that anyone recently wronged seek redress at the gates of the city and requesting the attendance of the latter upon his return.

It is puzzling that, given his own fear of slander, the Duke would want to denounce Angelo. He was initially motivated to select a deputy because of his anxiety about his own reputation (I.ii.39–43); the public exposure of his substitute's incompetence would appear to reflect badly on him. Vincentio is deeply disturbed by Lucio's slanders in III.ii, yet the Duke is also responsible for spreading rumors about his own absence. If he is so anxious to avoid slander, why does the Duke seem to promote it?

The Duke makes his most vehement denunciation of slander in Act IV, while lamenting the ruler's inability to avoid detraction. The great are represented as inextricably connected to defamation, which maintains a limpet-like hold on authority:

> O place and greatness! Millions of false eyes
> Are stuck upon thee: volumes of report
> Run with these false, and most contrarious quest
> Upon thy doings: thousand escapes of wit

Make thee the father of their idle dream
And rack thee in their fancies. (IV.i.60–5)

However, this association of slander with the ruler reverses from a juxtaposition of rumor and ruler to an identification of the Duke with defamation personified. Although the Duke's explicit meaning indicates that his subjects' surveillance and misrepresentation of their ruler threaten him, the allusion suggests his ability to spy on and defame *them*. The Arden edition (Shakespeare 1965: 99) notes the similarity of the metaphor in lines 60–2 to the description of Fame in Jonson's *Poetaster*:

Looke, how many plumes are plac't
On her huge corps, so many waking eyes
Sticke vnderneath: and (which may stranger rise
In the report) as many tongues shee beares,
As many mouthes, as many listning ears. (V.ii.85–9)

The eyes of a slanderous audience fixed on the Duke can also be read as eyes attached to, and looking out from, his own body. "[P]lace and greatness" are transformed into an allegorical figure of bad fame – defamation – in a description which presents authority as being covered with eyes, just as Fame is depicted by Jonson.[10] Strikingly, while Jonson uses this passage to condemn the lower-level magistrate Lupus who threatens both poet and the state, Shakespeare's handling of the allusion refers to the ruler himself. The Duke is not so much the victim of slander as its source.

The Duke's role as slanderer is most clearly presented in the last act of the play. When he returns undisguised to Vienna, Vincentio receives Isabella's accusations of Angelo with an apparently suspicious ear. He concludes that she has been "suborn'd against [A]ngelo's honour / In hateful practice" (V.i.109–10) and dismisses her valid claims as false imputations. She is consequently arrested for her defamation:

To prison with her! Shall we thus permit
A blasting and scandalous breath to fall
On him so near us? This needs must be a practice. (V.i.124–6)

The Duke proceeds to accuse Friar Lodowick (his disguised persona), Friar Peter, and Mariana, along with Isabella, of plotting to defame his deputy. He leaves the latter two in Angelo's hands to be punished: "stir not till you have well determin'd / Upon these slanderers" (v.i.257–8). The two women are accused of slander when they justly charge Angelo with wrongdoing; they are, in effect, slandered by being called slanderers. The irony here is that the Duke is behind this "practice" which results in the slandering of both his deputy as well as Mariana and Isabella. When Vincentio returns disguised as Friar Lodowick, he speaks the most destructive sedition in the play:

> My business in this state
> Made me a looker-on here in Vienna
> Where I have seen corruption boil and bubble
> Till it o'errun the stew: laws for all faults
> But faults so countenanc'd that the strong statutes
> Stand like the forfeits in a barber's shop,
> As much in mock as mark. (v.i.314–20)

Escalus, realizing the danger this speech poses to the established order, immediately calls for the Friar's arrest: "Slander to th'state!/ Away with him to prison!" (320–1).

What does the Duke – who throughout the play attests to his desire to avoid slander – gain by such a manifest self-slander? The result of his dramatic and defamatory epiphanies is to batter the majority of his subjects into submission and silence. By posing as a slanderer and promoting slander, the Duke maneuvers practically all of the characters present into positions of subservience: Angelo, Escalus, Isabella, and the Provost all ask for his pardon; and Mariana, Barnardine, and Claudio are completely indebted to him. If Vincentio's original intention in leaving Vienna was to reassert his authority, he would appear to be largely successful. The Duke's appointment of Angelo posed a threat of self-slander, but it was a carefully calculated risk. Vincentio clearly had no intentions of selecting a candidate who was conspicuously well-equipped for the job. All of Escalus' actions demonstrate that he is both a just and merciful ruler; in the Duke's absence, his expertise and compassion would have made him more popular than his superior.[11] Angelo, on the other hand, was bound to be unpopular whether he succeeded, because he enforced the law too harshly, or failed, as he did. The deputy's service falls so short of even Vincentio's abilities that the latter's authority is enhanced profoundly by comparison.

Vincentio's control over his subjects appears so absolute as to approach omniscience. Angelo articulates this sense of the Duke's power when his guilt is discovered near the play's end.

> O my dread lord,
> I should be guiltier than my guiltiness
> To think that I can be undiscernible,
> When I perceive your Grace, like power divine,
> Hath looked upon my passes. (V.i.364–8)

The ruler, as God's temporal representative, is endowed with a transcendent authority; the Duke's disguise as a Friar, which allows him omniscience over his subjects, serves to emphasize this point. The Duke possesses something of the eclipsing authority of divine power that Puttenham ascribes to satiric poets; he describes them as

> disguised persons vnder the shape of Satyres as who would say, these terrene and base gods being conuersant with mans affaires, and spiers out of all their secret faults: had some great care ouer man, & desired by good admonitions to reforme the euill of their life, and to bring the bad to amendment by those kinde of preachings, whereupon the Poets inuentors of the deuise were called Satyristes. (Puttenham 1936: 31)

Vincentio is a kind of "terrene god" who spies out and exposes the vices of his subjects and his substitute. While the apparent function of his role as "satyriste" is the reformation of vice in Vienna, the Duke's ultimate motive in using the power of satiric exposure is to reaffirm his own authority.

James I was an eloquent and frequent articulator of the relationship of monarch to deity. In a February 1604–5 charge to the judges and justices of the peace, he describes the ruler's divine right: "the kinge's Matie, as it were inheritabel & descended from god, hathe absolutelye monarchicall power annexed inseperablye to his Crowne & diademe" (Hawarde 1894: 188). This privilege gave the king, according to James, absolute power in the reign and reformation of his kingdom:

> his Ma$^{tie's}$ pleasure & express Charge ys that the vulgar shall not leape into his throne & reforme any contempte herein, but shall Complaine to the maiestrate & he shall prouyd for yt, and his Matie will exacte accounte at his handes [from officers who neglect] . . . his Ma$^{tie's}$ pleasure herein. (Hawarde 1894: 162)

James clearly felt it the king's sole right to criticize the state. In his *Basilikon Doron* (1599) he identifies a fault common to all of his subjects: "which is, to judge and speake rashly of their Prince"

(James I, 1918: 27). This comment comes at the end of a list of reproofs of his subjects' shortcomings, in which, as he explains to Prince Henry,

> I have not spared to be something Satyricke, in touching well quickly the faults in all the estates of my kingdom: But I protest before God, I doe it with the fatherly loue that I owe to them all; onely hating their vices, whereof there is a good number of honest men free in every estate. (James I 1918: 27)

Although verse satire exposing flaws in the government might be transgressive, the ruler is licensed to satirize the vices of his subjects. In James' view, the king's position enables him to criticize his people and discourage their criticism of him.

However, the Duke's determination to expose every character on the stage extends the ruler's right to criticize beyond his ability to justify it. In so doing, Vincentio completes his humiliation of his on-stage audience, transforming them from welcoming spectators into chastened criminals. By silencing his subjects, the Duke eradicates not only the slander, but also the affirmation of his actions. When the audience itself is deliberately put in the position of the disgraced criminal, it has no choice but to identify with the criminal against the ruler. Foucault's comments on public execution are applicable to this moment of public humiliation, in which the spectators not only sympathize with the criminal, but become him: "out of the ceremony of public execution, out of that uncertain festival in which violence was instantaneously reversible, it was [the solidarity between audience and criminal] much more than the sovereign power that was likely to emerge with redoubled strength" (Foucault 1979: 63).

The monarch's right to "satirize" his realm must also stop short of intentionally appointing corrupt officials. In fact, according to James, the ruler's ability to restrain popular criticism of the state is dependent upon the appointment of just magistrates who will address such grievances. Officers who fail to fulfill their duties by allowing subjects' complaints to go unredressed – and who thus run the risk of encouraging disparagement of the state – will be called into account by the king. Contemporary legal theory also suggests that the ruler's right to criticize and expose did not include the ability to slander his realm by the selection of incompetent substitutes. In the early seventeenth century, libels of a magistrate or a public person were perceived by the Star Chamber to jeopardize the security of the state: "'Let all men . . . take heed how they complayne in words against any magistrate for they are gods'" (Holdsworth 1927–66, v: 208–9). In the case *de Libellis Famosis* Coke states that libel against a magistrate is a greater offense than against a private person:

for it concerns not only the breach of the peace, but also the scandal of Government; for what greater scandal of Government can there be than to have corrupt or wicked magistrates to be appointed and constituted by the King to govern his subjects under him? And greater imputation to the State cannot be, than to suffer such corrupt men to sit in the sacred seat of justice, or to have any meddling in or concerning the administration of justice. (Coke 1907: 251)

Ferdinando Pulton makes a similar observation in his *De pace regnis et regni* (1609):

libelling, secret slandring or defaming . . . against a publicke magistrate . . . is a great sca[n]dal & offence to the king, his chief magistrates, & the whole gouernment of the realm, to assigne such an officer to rule & gouern others, who himself is void of gouernme[n]t, & shal deserue to be impeached with such crimes as he shalbe taxed with, or shall be imputed vnto him by such an infamous libell. (Pulton 1609: B.2^{v})

Although the gist of these statements is that this serious offense is the fault of the slanderer, both Coke and Pulton seem to suggest that the real threat to the peace of the realm lies with the king who appoints an incompetent magistrate.

In naming and then condemning an incompetent deputy, the Duke opens up his government to the slanders he himself articulates in Act v. As Coke's and Pulton's comments quoted above suggest, corrupt rulers who appoint incompetent magistrates *deserve* to be slandered. *Measure for Measure* presents a critique of the state's willingness to manipulate and undermine its servants – particularly susceptible to state slander because they draw their authority from the state – for its own ends by demonstrating that this practice ultimately subverts the authority of the state. Vincentio's subsequent condemnation of Lucio for "Slandering a prince" (v.i.521) calls into question his own defamatory practice. Angelo is punished for hypocrisy, for failing to chastise in himself the vices he so vehemently prosecuted in others.[12] By the doctrine of *lex talionis* that Vincentio sets out in the course of the play, the Duke must also correct his own vice when castigating Lucio's slanders. His ultimate goal – to reassert his authority and reputation in Vienna, "And yet [his] nature never in the fight / To do in slander" (I.iii.42–3) – fails in his alienation of the very spectators he wished to impress.

Thus, just as the "fantastical Duke of dark corners" effects the several exposures of his subjects, Lucio's presence also serves to expose the Duke. Vincentio's ability to spy out men's secret faults seems to be aptly described by Puttenham, but we must remember that the passage quoted above referred to poets, not rulers. Lucio is equally capable of discovering the Duke's "secret faults." He does so figuratively when he claims that the disguised Duke is no true friar (V.i.261–3), and then literally when he unmasks "Friar Lodowick" (V.i.349–53).[13] Finally, Lucio's extremely harsh punishment for slander, not fornication, exposes and calls into question the Duke's own defamatory practices while raising questions about the punishment owing to the more dangerous slanderer.

Lucio's slanders of the Duke are dangerous precisely because they ultimately expose the danger of the Duke's slanders. In contrast to Spenser and Jonson, Shakespeare does not imagine the poet as a servant of the state, but as a competitor for definition of and control over defamation. If the state insists on defining slander, including the work of poets, as always destructive, then it must of necessity condemn its own deployment of defamation. Here the state, not the poet, damns itself in attempting to fix a stable negative definition of slander. *Measure for Measure* shows that the state's dramatic slander is more hazardous than the poet's. In fact, attempts to discredit the slanderous aspects of the theatre could rebound against the state by calling into question the ruler's own use of theatrical power to expose and punish. The Duke's attempt to ballast his authority by means of theatrical slander is undermined by his punishment of Lucio for the latter's slanders. In its dramatization of the Duke's actions, *Measure for Measure* employs the state's own methods of exposure to censure the arbitrariness of its response to theatre and, in so doing, demonstrates that the instability of slander is just as likely to humiliate the perpetrator as his intended victim.

Conclusion

The point of this book has been not to replace the censorship paradigm with that of defamation, but rather to suggest that we situate the former within the latter and reconsider its significance in terms of a broader cultural context. I have been at pains to establish that defamation was a significant social concern in the early modern period, and by focusing on the works of three major contemporary authors I attempt to demonstrate the literary importance of defamation. What can we now conclude about the place of literature and literary representations of power relations between the poet and state once we locate them within a more complex understanding of responses to transgressive language in early modern England?

Let us return briefly to the literary representations of slander to begin an answer to this question. In their respective works, Spenser and Jonson both endeavor to preserve poetry from allegations of slander by establishing them as stable and diametrically opposed categories of good and evil in order to distinguish between the two. They also imagine a symbiotic relationship between the virtuous poet and the enlightened ruler which will provide a united front against slander. However, when they represent their works as meeting with official disapproval, both indirectly redefine this criticism as defamation in order to discredit it. On the one hand this is a rhetorically powerful move because it aims to legitimate their work in the face of "slanderous" attacks. On the other hand, however, the state can respond to such imputations by labeling this poetic criticism as libel, a charge that is difficult to shake, given the popular and legal associations of poetry with slander. Because Spenser and Jonson have insisted, as the state has, on the absolute evil of slander, once they fall into accusing the state of this absolute evil they become susceptible to charges of sedition. Ultimately, the state defines what constitutes legitimate or transgressive language, in spite of poets' claims to the contrary that they, as producers of virtuous discourse, should make this determination. Shakespeare avoids the logic of this pitfall by abandoning stable categories of virtuous and transgressive speech. In his representation the ruler, not the poet, attempts to maintain these binary categories in the face of the play's pragmatic, and accurate, assumption that both poets and rulers employ slander. When the Duke insists on the illegitimacy of slander by punishing Lucio so harshly he, more emphatically than Spenser and Jonson in similar circumstances, condemns himself.

But does this offer us any escape from the contingencies set up in the censorship model? If poetry is simply redefined as slander and reinscribed as transgressive language, is it not placed in the same situation of repression that censorship posits? One response would be the one Shakespeare offers, that the state's implication in slander prevents it from successfully suppressing it. But Shakespeare's model could also suggest that Vincentio emerges as the victor, not because he can criminalize Lucio's slanders, but because, in terms of realpolitik, he is the more successful slanderer. However, a better response would be to remember that the instability of slander's power makes it impossible to contain whether you authorize it or not. After all, the slanders the Duke deploys inadvertently include powerful charges against himself as well as others. He may be successful in silencing others' slanders against him by the end of the play, but silence does not necessarily convey compliance or respect. If the aim of the Duke's plot has been to resurrect and reinforce his authority, its success is unclear at the conclusion of the play. The Duke may have the last word, but what this really reveals is his failure to elicit responses from any of the characters, with the obvious and unwanted exception of Lucio, once his plot is disclosed. In Isabella's notable silence in the concluding scene we can read a refusal of the Duke's proposal; as the most virtuous character in the play, her rejection serves as a measure of the larger failure of his project to gain his subjects' respect.

When we turn to an assessment of defamation on the extra-literary social level, we find further evidence for the power of language that could be turned against the state and which eluded its control. Several recent studies have demonstrated the force defamation could exert by subjects against their superiors. In *The Pursuit of Stability*, Ian Archer argues that stability was maintained in the face of serious social tensions in late sixteenth-century London through the solidarity of interests of the city elite (the aldermen) and divisions among the middle and lower classes. However, the elite managed to maintain control in part through responding – even if only in minor and limited ways – to the concerns of the middle and lower classes. One powerful way in which apprentices made their grievances against foreign competition known was through the threat of riot and the circulation of libels.

> Once we appreciate that riot was a negotiating strategy, we may become sensitive to other means by which pressure was brought to bear upon the elite, and other ways in which the tensions in the civic polity were expressed. Libels, those "proclamations and trumpets of sedition" as one government minister put it in 1593, with the threat of action that they conveyed, were one such means . . . libels fulfilled their functions in encouraging the rulers of companies supported by the aldermanic elite to take action against strangers . . . libels might be seen as a mechanism, short of riot, by which the aldermen were reminded of their functions in the markets. (Archer 1991: 7–8)

Anxiety about the power of libels can be measured by the 1593 Privy Council order authorizing "the use of torture in the discovery of libellers" (Archer 1991: 8). While the balance of power clearly remained with the elite, the lower classes were able to force a response to their complaints through the circulation of texts deemed transgressive – being termed libels – but containing legitimate concerns that the upper echelons could not afford to ignore.

Alastair Bellany's essay "'Raylinge Rymes and Vaunting Verse'" focuses more specifically on the threat that defamatory speeches and texts posed to the stability of the political order.[1] While Bellamy limits his analysis to the early seventeenth century, he acknowledges the development of political verse out of local traditions of mocking rhymes in the sixteenth century (Bellany 1993: 287–8). A striking characteristic of verse libels is the fluidity of media with which they circulated. A scrivener named Willoughby, under questioning in 1628 for his association with John Felton, the Duke of Buckingham's assassin, was asked how a couplet predicting the assassination came to be among his papers:

> Willoughby described the passage of this couplet from the street to his desk. Lawrence Naylor, an illiterate baker's boy, had heard the rhyme several times and had memorised it, and then passed it on to one Daniel Watkins, who in turn related it orally to Willoughby. The Suffolk cleric John Rous received a

variant version of the couplet in conversation . . . The brevity and form of the couplet allowed it to circulate across social and literacy boundaries, and in a variety of social settings. (Bellany 1993: 288)

Bellany notes that libels circulated primarily in manuscript form; manuscripts were often left in public places such as the Royal Exchange or St. Paul's, where they could be read, picked up and copied (Bellany 1993: 291).

From London, copies of libels could reach the provinces along developing channels of information distribution . . . Professional and amateur newsletters helped to spread these verses into the provinces . . . It is possible that some verses may have been copied out and sold by those stationers who specialised in selling manuscript copies of banned works like Thomas Scott's *Vox Populi*. (Bellany 1993: 291)

Social occasions also provided opportunities for communicating libels: the passing of a libel around the dinner table, reading groups for the exchange of news, or the circulation of commonplace books among friends (Bellany 1993: 291–2).

The ubiquity of libels insured a certain impact and forced official response. James I felt the need to respond to an anti-Spanish verse libel with a poem of his own, although it is not clear that ruler had the last word in this matter (Bellany 1993: 294). In the case of Buckingham's death, Bellany argues that

Libels reflected and created a moral universe in which Buckingham's assassination became both imaginable and desirable. It is hard to avoid the conclusion that their circulation must have contributed, along with parliamentary remonstrance against the duke, to the tide of real and mimetic violence that eventually culminated in the murder of the favourite. (Bellany 1993: 304)

Official accounts of Felton and his trial labored to criminalize him and Charles ordered his body to be hung in chains on the highest tower in Portsmouth to frighten supporters (Bellany 1993: 306). However,

Attempts through punitive ritual and poetic responses to portray Felton as a murderer, or at least raise the issue of the morality of the crime, were subverted by libels which ignored the moral issues of assassination to ruminate instead on the public good that had resulted. (Bellany 1993: 307)

In the public forum of opinion, unauthorized and oppositional verse could circulate, challenge official claims, and garner popular support, demonstrating that the determination of discursive legitimacy is conferred by the audience, not the state.

While censorship of a wide range of texts increased in the tumultuous years before the civil war, it was impossible to suppress the circulation of political opinion. Drawing on the work of Christopher Hill, Bellany contends that "surreptitiously circulating" verse libel "escaped the 'conventions of political discourse' imposed by censorship . . . Their wide distribution among regions and classes allowed them an important role in politicising the nation, expressing and creating discontent, and eroding political legitimacy" (Bellany 1993: 309). His argument concludes with the suggestion that libels contributed significantly to the deteriorating political climate of the early seventeenth century which ultimately resulted in the overthrow and beheading of Charles I.

For the early modern period, defamation was a central and powerful force affecting the lives of English citizens regardless of rank or gender. While numerous official mechanisms, including the censorship of literary texts, existed to control a range of transgressive language, the instability of this discursive threat made it ultimately impossible to silence. Models of censorship focus on the exercise of state power; in so doing, they ignore what a defamatory model reveals: the elusive power of discourse. In the increasingly unstable period leading up to the Civil War, slander had demonstrably political repercussions; not only was the government unable to control slander for its own purposes – which it continued to attempt to do – but it was ultimately helpless to protect itself from the damage slander can inflict. Spenser and Jonson exercise a certain amount of agency in the context of the struggle to define legitimate discourse. In their representations of power relations with the state, they could argue for the superior authority of their words. Yet, to the extent that these poets sought official agreement with, if not approval for their views, they ceded power away from the authority they were trying to establish. Shakespeare, however, acknowledges the unstable power of defamation; his oblique condemnation of the Duke's punishment of Lucio indicates that the criminalization of poetry does not result in increased authority for the ruler. Evidence from political and social historians of libel ballasts Shakespeare's claim. If attempts were made in the early modern period to discredit poetry by associating it with defamation, the subversive potential of libels linked poets to a discursive power that eluded official containment and successfully challenged the state's authority.

Notes

INTRODUCTION: CENSORSHIP VERSUS SLANDER

1 I must acknowledge that I am guilty of referring to the complex, fractured and competing branches of early modern governance by the flattening and misleadingly monolithic term "state" for ease of argument at many points in this book. When discussing the specifics of slander law, I attend to the conflicts and differences contained within the legal and ruling systems. However, in general discussions and especially in analyses of the literary texts, I adopt this unsatisfactory term to signify governance in general, following the lead of vague and/or idealized literary representations of ruling authority.

2 The increase in defamation cases in this period, in both secular and ecclesiastical courts, is noted by numerous authorities: see Milsom 1981: 386; Helmholz 1985: lxxxvi; Baker 1990: 500–1; Ingram 1987: 292–3.

3 Sheila Lambert comments that "the belief that the only relationship there could be between government and printers was one of repression is proving very hard to get rid of" and notes that there has been a "new upsurge in writings based on the old assumption that [there was] a government policy of all-pervasive censorship intended to prevent all expression of unorthodox opinion . . . In my view, studies such as these are based on a mistaken premise for there never was any intention or attempt on the part of James I and Charles I to 'suppress all criticism'" (Lambert 1987: 1). She suggests that Siebert's outdated argument may have contributed to these unfounded conclusions: "Patterson relied for the history of censorship on F. S. Siebert . . . it is unfortunate that this work, which was essentially completed in 1930, is still treated as standard" (Lambert 1987: 23 n. 1). Thanks to Peter Blayney for bringing Lambert's work to my attention.

4 This argument raises the questions: who are the readers to which she refers and, given the instability of language, how can they all read in the same way? Why would writers willingly participate in an agreement with these readers and what interests do they have in common?

5 David Loades' essay "The Theory and Practice of Censorship in Sixteenth-Century England" is exceptional in its explicit linkage of the origins of censorship with laws relating to defamation and blasphemy (Loades 1991: 97). However, he is primarily concerned with general press censorship, not

literature, and does not develop further connections between slander law and the control of texts, or speech. In the introduction to his *Lost Plays of Shakespeare's Age*, C. J. Sisson (1936) also briefly situates the suppression of plays and jigs within the context of libel law.

6 Unlike scholarship focused on censorship, which often has to speculate on issues because the evidence has been destroyed, an examination from the perspective of slander law reveals that many contentions about defamation survive intact in poetic representations that, nevertheless, do not constitute defamation in and of themselves.

1 THE PARADOX OF SLANDER

1 The Star Chamber makes a distinction in criminal and tortious defamation, defining written defamations as the more serious offense. But while that court held written defamation to be more dangerous, it was actually more concerned about the status of the victim and the disturbance which resulted, or could potentially result, from defaming a person of importance. This is evident even in the common law redress for slander; the *scandalum magnatum* statute influenced later slander law in that members of the nobility who were defamed could successfully pursue a case that would not bear an action for a commoner (March 1647: 132[mispaginated for 134]–6). While sexual slander of a common woman, if considered actionable at all under the common law, was seen as a tort which could be redressed by the award of damages, verbal imputations about the queen's sexual reputation constituted sedition, which was punishable by death (Samaha 1975). The problem was not so much written defamation versus spoken but the seriousness of the disruption caused by the words. If the state thought libel more dangerous than slander, it also thought defamation of a nobleman more serious than that of a commoner.

2 The *American Heritage Dictionary of Indo-European Roots* lists two separate entries for *bha*, "to shine" and "to speak," without articulating a connection, although their meanings and development seem related. For an acknowledged connection between similar meanings, see *deik*, "to show, pronounce solemnly," from which digit (pointer, finger) and diction (speech) derive. Thanks to Alex Sens for helping me make this connection.

3 Helmholz translates "ut sic saltem ei purgatio indicatur" as "by reason of which purgation at least is awarded to him" (Helmholz 1985: xiv); the term "award" carries a positive connotation which is not, I think, intended in this context, since purgation is an ordeal one must undergo to clear one's name of charges. I take *indicatur* as a passive form of *indico* (xi) which carries the sense "To impose, enjoin, inflict . . . to impose a penalty" (Lewis 1977). Maclean translates this phrase "with the result that he is obliged at least to resort to compurgation" (Maclean 1992: 189).

4 Though, in practice, most plaintiffs alleged that the words were false and apparently only false imputations were actionable (Helmholz 1985: xxx–xxxii).

5 This is in no way a critical evaluation of the development of slander law in sixteenth-century England such as legal historians of the subject are wont to make. For example, in discussing the differentiation of libel and slander, J. H. Baker opines that the "distinction is not very useful, nor very easy to apply in an age of gramophone records, television, and magnetic recording. Although scholars have found some diversion in its intricacies, it bears the unsightly scars of a historical accident[!]" (Baker 1990: 508). Rather, I am interested in investigating the *structure* of defamation, and its significance for early modern English culture.

6 It would be misleading to omit mention that for both the common and the ecclesiastical law, truth was almost always a defense; that is, if the speaker could prove the words spoken were true, they were not considered defamatory. However, in the case of libel as developed in Star Chamber (which I will discuss later) truth was NOT a defense. While the redresses for slander essentially fulfilled their function, the unstable nature of the offense made the development and enforcement of these remedies quite problematic.

7 The ecclesiastical jurisdiction over slander only extended to its spiritual consequences; in its redress it was concerned with the reintegration of the guilty party into the Christian community after appropriate penance had been done. The redress aimed also to restore the reputation of the person defamed, but this injury was not understood as having temporal, that is, financial, consequences.

8 I am arguing from the evidence as presented by Helmholz in his extensive study of slander cases in English ecclesiastical, local, and royal courts in the period leading up to 1600. J. H. Baker, in his *Introduction to English Legal History*, contends that from the inception of its redress the common law defined defamation solely in terms of the resulting damage, and not in terms of the words spoken (Baker 1990: 498–500). While I am not in a position to adjudicate between these two eminent historians, I tend towards Professor Helmholz's account both because he has made it the focus of a separate study and because the variety and number of materials he consulted in compiling his study supply him, I suspect, with a more complete picture of the injury.

9 For a discussion of the incoherence in the development of common law slander, with regard to both the ecclesiastical and Star Chamber definitions, see Milsom 1981: 385–8.

10 The ecclesiastical courts were seen as competing with the common law courts in a variety of jurisdictions during the turbulent years of Henrician reform (Helmholz 1985: lxxix). However, with regard to defamation, the establishment of the common law redress did not divert too much business away from the church courts. In fact, both forms of redress enjoyed a considerable increase in business in the course of the sixteenth century (Sharpe 1980: 3–4; Helmholz 1985: xlv).

11 I do not mean to suggest here that slander was unique in this respect; much of common law, as its name implies, is precedent-based. Additionally, the

early sixteenth century saw a great deal of legal innovation, as J. H. Baker points out:

actions on the case for not paying debts, for converting goods, and for breach of promise, were all sanctioned by the King's Bench in the same thirty-year period [in which actions for slander developed]. It was therefore an opportune time to introduce an action for words. (Baker 1990: 498)

My purpose in emphasizing innovation in slander law is to show how it contributed to the problematic structure of the offense.

12 "It is conceivable that the two alternate rules of lenient or harsh construction were used by the judges to justify, and later to interpret, cases which had been decided one way or the other on more equitable grounds. There are hints of this in the reports" (Helmholz 1985: xciv–xcv). Baker advances a different account of the *mitior sensus* doctrine, in which he argues it was a judicial strategy for abating the number of cases coming to the central courts (Baker 1990: 500–2); for examples of both construction *in mitiori sensu* and *in malem partem*, see Baker and Milsom 1986: 637–47). Helmholz disagrees with Baker's conclusions (Helmholz 1985: xcii–xcv).

13 See also Baker 1990: 500–1, who discusses what he sees as attempts to abate the "flood" of slander actions; and see Sharpe 1980: 3–4 and Milsom 1981: 379, 386.

14 Elsewhere, Coke takes an opposing view; in summarizing a collection of slander cases, he expresses the hope that they "will deter men from subjecting themselves to actions in which damages and costs are to be recovered . . . for words, which are but wind" (Baker and Milsom 1986: 642). The contradiction may be accounted for, perhaps, by distinguishing between tort cases, which focus on financial loss, and criminal cases, which threaten the public order. Coke may be suggesting that in the former cases words are merely wind, while in the latter they result in serious consequences. Nevertheless this is a difficult distinction to maintain, since the same words might result in a brawl or financial loss.

15 For an example of the kind of disruption imputations against honor could pose for local government, see A. H. Smith's *County and Court: Government and Politics in Norfolk, 1558–1603* (1974: 181–92).

16 The claim I make that the state operated by means of institutionalized slander cannot be completely supported by the fact that true accusations could constitute libel, for in the normal course of legal procedure state-sanctioned accusations of crime would not be seen to pose a threat to the peace, even if such charges did result in violence. However, my point here is to show that accusations made and punishments inflicted by the state functioned structurally as slander; that is, the aim of such methods was to humiliate individuals publicly by means of assertions of criminality. Official attempts to define as slander private imputations against citizens or the state show that the Star Chamber was concerned to criminalize defamation in order to distinguish it from state practice. The Privy Council was anxious to control defamation by deploring the power of language to criticize and expose, both because slander constituted in part

state power, and because it was also a weapon that could be turned against the state.

17 I want to acknowledge that while some of Foucault's observations about seventeenth- and eighteenth-century France are applicable to late sixteenth- and early seventeenth-century England, there are some significant differences. Primarily, the British legal system, founded on the common law, was quite distinct from continental systems based on the Roman or civil law; the most significant dissimilarity, for the purposes of my argument, is the respective attitudes toward trial and torture. Foucault notes the greater importance of torture in France (and most of Europe), where the legal procedure up until the punishment was kept secret and torture publicly enacted the private trial (Foucault 1979: 35–47). Because British criminal proceedings were open to the public and relied on a peer jury, public opinion and judgment were brought in as part of the judicial process. While the capital or corporal punishments of criminals in England were painful, they were not understood as the torture Foucault describes which, theoretically, did not exist in England under the common law (see Hanson [1991] who challenges this claim). However, since I am interested only in the aspects of humiliation in Foucault's account – which, due to the public nature of the British criminal process, were even more salient – I feel justified in relying on his analysis on this point.

18 A copy of the 1570 edition of Foxe's book was commanded to be placed in every English church, along with the Bible (Foxe 1870, 1: 64).

19 For a related and more rigorous discussion of the instability of audience reception with regard to issues of authorial intention, subversion and the market for plays in the seventeenth century, see Burt (1988).

20 While Stephen Greenblatt (1973) focuses, to good effect, on the plasticity of Ralegh's self-presentation in his life and two treason trials, one could argue that the state shows a similar ingenuity in fabricating and manipulating the charges against him.

21 It should be noted that being at the mercy of an angry king did not prevent Ralegh from criticizing his ruler. Janet Clare notes that his *History of the World* was recalled by James in 1614, even though it had been licensed:

> According to Chamberlain in his letter to Carleton, the reason for its suppression was that it had been "too sawcie in censuring princes." Raleigh had presented several portraits of weak or dissolute rulers, but one in particular came a little too close to common perceptions of the King. The parallel between James and Ninias, who succeeded the magnificent Queen Semiramis and who was "esteemed no man of warre at all, but altogether feminine and subjected to ease and delicacie", is unmistakable. Unwisely, Raleigh had compared the early years of James's sovereignty unfavourably with the reign of Elizabeth. (Clare 1990: 154)

Rather than characterize this veiled criticism as unwise, I suggest it is a clever strategy on Ralegh's part to repay in kind James' slanders against him. The fact that James recognized the imputation and that contemporaries understood the nature of the conflict reveal a measure of the text's success.

22 See also the section on eclogues: "Poets deuised the Eglogue . . . [so as]

vnder the vaile of homely persons, and in rude speeches to insinuate and glaunce at greater matters, and such as perchance had not bene safe to haue beene disclosed in any other sort" (Puttenham 1936: 38).

23 The matter was apparently settled in 1610; the chief actors were to be

> committed to the Fleet, led through Westminster Hall with papers, and there be set on the pillory, and afterwards to be whipped under the pillory; also to be set in the pillory at the assizes in Lincolnshire and acknowledge their offences, and ask God and the Earl forgiveness, and then to be whipped under the pillory, and to pay 300£ a piece fine, and be bound to good behavior before enlargement. That Sir Edward Dymock who was privy and consenting to the offences aforesaid be committed to the Fleet during the King's pleasure and pay 1,000£ fine. (*Royal Commission of Historical Manuscripts* 1872: 57)

Dymock, who was certainly the fomenter of the plot, is fined more but spared the physical pain and public humiliation of the punishment inflicted on the actual actors.

24 In perusing a list of documents from the Tower with the antiquary, Elizabeth is reported by Lambarde to have hesitated over those pertaining to Richard II's reign and said "'I am Richard II. know ye not that?' W.L. [replied] 'Such a wicked imagination was determined and attempted by a most unkind Gent. the most adorned creature that ever your Majestie made.' Her Majestie [responded] 'He that will forget God, will also forget his benefactors; this tragedy was played 40^{tie} times in open streets and houses.'" See Peter Ure's introduction to the Arden *Richard II* (Shakespeare 1961: lix). Leeds Barroll (1988) argues against using this anecdote as evidence that the state found the theatre subversive. While I agree that other historical narratives must be examined before drawing conclusions about Lambarde's account, I believe that the documents set out in this chapter suggest that the Privy Council was concerned about theatrical impersonation, especially of persons of rank. Elizabeth's claim that "this tragedie was played 40^{tie} times" is surely an exaggeration, but one which registers a clear anxiety during a time of social unrest about being impersonated in the figure of a deposed king. Barroll does not disprove that dramatic impersonation threatens the state, he shows that the written word was held to pose a greater threat. He demonstrates that some of the conspirators responsible for commissioning the performance of *Richard II* were punished while the players were not; it makes perfect sense that the state condemned those who used the drama for seditious purposes, and ignored the players who were merely hired and performed the play without a certifiably treasonous intent. However, when the play is a manifestly slanderous one, as it is in the *Lincoln v. Dymock* case, both the actors and the instigator are harshly punished.

2 ALLEGORIES OF DEFAMATION IN *THE FAERIE QUEENE*, BOOKS IV–VI

1 Elizabeth was noted for her attempts to smooth over the conflicts resulting from the Reformation in her quest to forge a unified Church of England.

"Prince of peace" alludes to Isaiah's messianic prophecy (9:5) and emphasizes Elizabeth's divine mission as queen. Additionally, she resisted military aggression, much to the chagrin of the radical Protestant faction at court who urged, unsuccessfully, an intensification of the war effort against Spain (Norbrook 1984: 128–9, 125–31 *passim*, see also Bradshaw 1988: 162).

2 Joyce Sexton points out that Ate possesses traits traditionally associated with slander and envy (Sexton 1978: 30–2), and that these emotions are antithetical to love: "That detraction is the weapon of her choice serves to point up the power of slander over love" (Sexton 1978: 31).

3 Hamilton notes that the "ympes" mentioned here are the Argonauts. The "ragged monuments" (IV.i.21) which hang on the walls of Ate's abode record the strife "of the dreadfull discord, which did driue / The noble *Argonauts* to outrage fell, / That each of life sought others to depriue" (IV.I.23); Hamilton points out that their conflict was ended by Orpheus.

4 In the "Excuses (Confessions)" chapter of his *Allegories of Reading*, Paul de Man suggests an analogous account of the radical areferentiality of slander. This analysis is included in his discussion of the different versions Rousseau offers of the "Purloined Ribbon" episode. The story is simple: as a young servant Rousseau steals a ribbon; when it is found in his possession, he accuses Marion, a fellow servant, of having stolen it and giving it to him. In the *Confessions*, Rousseau manages to excuse the denial of the theft, but fails to justify defaming Marion. He acknowledges in the *Fourth Reverie* his failure to face the moral consequences of slander: "To lie for one's own advantage is deceit, to lie for the benefit of another is fraudulent, to lie in order to harm is slander; it is the worst kind of lie" (de Man 1979: 285, note 7). In coming to terms with his injury to Marion, Rousseau offers this explanation of his accusation: "Je m'excusai sur le premier objet qui s'offrit" (de Man 1979: 288). de Man understands this excuse to mean that Rousseau did not intend to slander Marion, she merely came to mind at the moment he was called on to confess.

> But the use of a vocabulary of contingency ("le premier objet qui s'offrit") within an argument of causality is arresting and disruptive, for the sentence is phrased in such a way as to allow for a complete disjunction between Rousseau's desires and interests and the selection of this particular name. Marion just happened to be the first thing that came to mind; any other name, any other word, any other sound or noise could have done just as well and Marion's entry in the discourse is a mere effect of chance. (de Man 1979: 288)

The accusation of Marion is finally only a sound without meaning which is falsely interpreted by its hearers. The agency of slander is moved from the speaker to the hearer.

> As a fiction, the statement is innocuous and the error harmless; it is the misguided reading of the error as theft or slander, the refusal to admit that fiction is fiction, the stubborn resistance to the "fact," obvious by itself, that language is entirely free with regard to referential meaning and can posit whatever its grammar allows it to say, which leads to the transformation of random error into injustice. (de Man 1979: 293)

5 In his analysis of the Bon/Malfont scene, Jonathan Goldberg sees Spen-

ser's depiction of a poet punished by the ruler as his capitulation to the queen's will.

> The substitute name [of Malfont for Bonfont] represents the poet's submission to the truth vested in the authoritative figure of the ruler, Mercilla, and it translates a social reality, that the poet's words are at the sovereign's command . . . Trial and punishment are exactly what Mercilla commands, and to be brought to trial is tantamount to condemnation. (Goldberg 1983: 1–2)

Goldberg somewhat paradoxically sees this submission as empowering the poet: "Spenser seems to want his reader to believe that his tongue, like Bon/Malfont's, is at the royal command, and that his text is 'privileged' to speak the truths Elizabeth wanted to hear" (Goldberg 1983: 3). I would argue that Spenser raises the possibility of Malfont only to raze it, that is, reject it as a valid view of the true poet. In accordance with Sidney's defense of poetry, one must first acknowledge the criticism leveled against the poet before successfully refuting it. However, in dismissing Malfont as a false poet, Spenser does not suggest that the true poet finds his source of inspiration in the queen's authority. As I will contend in my discussion of Book VI, Spenser locates his ability to speak the truth, not in his submission to the monarch, but in the poet's association with virtue, which enables him to teach the ruler the "truth."

6 "*Although the private man or magistrate [i.e., public figure] be dead at the time of the making of the libel, yet it is punishable:* for in the one case it stirs up others of the same family, blood or society, to revenge, and to break the peace, and in the other the libeller traduces and slanders the State and Government, which dies not" (Coke 1907: 251). While Mary was a queen, she was also deemed an enemy of England, which raises the question of whether Spenser's account could constitute defamation or even sedition; there is some irony in James' implicitly charging Spenser for sedition in depicting Mary as guilty of it. See Manning for a discussion of how Coke shaped the definition of sedition (Manning 1980: 116–19).

7 While I agree with Roche that this incident focuses on the issue of honor, I would like to complicate his argument by suggesting that Belphoebe, usually depicted as the locus of chaste and honorable behavior, here shares attributes with characters embodying dishonor.

8 Roche credits Allan H. Gilbert with this insight (Roche 1964: 142–3). In the note to IV.vii.37 in his edition of *The Faerie Queene*, A. C. Hamilton argues: "Since Timias' name signifies honour, dishonour brings death; hence he is seen as a ghost, 41.4, viii 12.7." He cites Roche who makes a similar point (Roche 1964: 145–6).

9 Historians have recently begun to re-examine Spenser's attitudes towards Ireland as evidenced not only in Book V, but in the *View of the Present State of Ireland.* A debate has sprung up between Nicholas Canny and Ciaran Brady over whether the policies advocated by Spenser in *A View*, and less centrally in *The Faerie Queene*, were in accord with contemporary advice about colonizing Ireland or represent a distinctive and cruel divergence from informed opinion (Brady and Canny 1988). It is not my interest here to resolve this argument, but rather to refocus the findings of

Canny and Brady on the representation of Grey in Book v. Their discussion of Spenser's motivations for writing *A View* also sheds light on his shaping of the Artegall/Grey narrative.

10 I have found what appears to be a draft of Grey's instructions from Elizabeth upon his appointment as Lord Deputy:

> And whereas o^{r} subiectes of that contreys birthe have as we are enformed, conceaved that we have a determinacon as it were to roote them oute with an intencon to place there o^{r} subiects borne in this Realme: we would have ye seeke by all the meanes that yo^{w} can to remove that false impression wrought in them by certaine seditious and ill disposde p[er]sons that would be glad to worrke a divorce betwene vs and o^{r} subiects there: whereas in truthe we being interessae [?] alike in o^{r} subiects of bothe these o^{r} Realmes, doe carie like affection to them bothe vnles throughe their vnnaturall and vndutifull dealing and by having intelligence wth forraine princes, as lately c^{r}taine of them have had, they shall geve vs iuste cause to the Contrarye. (PRO SP 12/134 626–7)

While she is concerned to protect herself from seditious complaints, Elizabeth nevertheless leaves open the possibility of hostile action against the Irish if they resist British rule. Again we see the strategy of deflecting slander by shifting culpability from the state to its antagonists.

11 The resentment that the Old English settlers felt for the New greatly influenced Elizabeth's Irish policies and resulted in the recall of a Lord Deputy more than once.

> [A]s the Old English saw it, their very survival as a privileged elite depended upon their ability to frustrate the intentions of the New English, and the only means that they could see to achieving this was to seek to discredit all New English servitors in the eyes of the queen. The severe measures taken by Arthur Lord Grey de Wilton in the suppression of the rebellions in both Munster and the Pale provided the Old English with an ideal subject on which to base their allegations . . . The essential point being made was that no conspiracy existed [among the inhabitants of the Pale], that the Old English lords (who were well disposed towards the crown) were being goaded into rebellion by the harsh, ill-advised, and frequently illegal actions of English officials and soldiers whose only concern was self-advancement. (Canny 1983: 13)

12 PRO SP 63/94(4). This letter is written in an italic hand, probably by Lord Grey and not by Spenser who wrote Grey's correspondence in a beautiful secretary hand. I have preserved the spelling and most of the contractions, but have supplied punctuation to help make sense of the structure of his syntax, typical of the early modern English elliptical style.

13 Grey's requests to be relieved of his duty were in fact based on his realization that Elizabeth would never supply him with the men, money, or moral support needed to pursue his rigorous and harsh plans to subjugate the Irish. Spenser's representation of Artegall as thwarted in the implementation of his policies is in this sense accurate.

14

> Therewith Sir *Guyon* left his first emprise, [i.e., Furor]
> And turning to that woman, fast her hent
> By the hoare lockes, that hong before her eyes,
> And to the ground her threw: yet n'ould she stent
> Her bitter rayling and foule reuilement,
> But still prouokt her sonne to wreake her wrong;

But nathelesse he did her still torment,
And catching hold of her vngratious tong,
Thereon an yron lock did fasten firme and strong.

Then when as vse of speach was from her reft,
With her two crooked handes she signes did make,
And beckned him, the last helpe she had left:
But he that last left helpe away did take.
And both her hands fast bound vnto a stake,
That she note stirre. Then gan her sonne to flie
Full fast away, and did her quite forsake;
But *Guyon* after him in haste did hie,
And soone him ouertooke in sad perplexitie. (II.iv.12–13)

15 In *Solon His Folly*, a 1594 treatise on settling Ireland, Richard Beacon, a former attorney of the province of Munster, discusses "occasion" in a defamatory context in Book III, chapter 4 entitled "*occasions and causes of all declinations, and first of occasions malitiously suggested*":

so the declination of this polliticke bodie groweth partely by occasions, and partely from the malice and corruption of the subiect, as from the vnnatural distemperature of that body. (Beacon 1594: 73)

Further on in Book III, chapter 9, he touches on circumstances where occasion is linked with lack of support for a reforming officer:

Occasions of decline are then given, when Magistrates placed for reformation of any Countrie or province, are not supported and countenaunced during the time of their governement.

SOLON: If princes, Kings, and States, shall not publikely grace, countenaunce, and support all governoures and Magistrates by them placed for reformation of any province or nation during the time of their government, the subiects shal take thereby occasion of rebelling . . . What governoures wer there, that wer found so vnskilful in their charge?

EPIMENIDES: A late deputie of *Salamina* [Ireland], whose name here I passe over with silence, for that I may not say, *honoris causa nomino.* But O you governoures, Princes, Kings, and Emperours, whatsoever, countenaunce all inferiour governoures and magistrates placed for the reformation of any nation or province . . . Lastly countenaunce Magistrate placed for reformation; for with *David,* he is placed to fight with a beare after a lion, with a Giant after a beare, [etc.] . . . They must fight with infamie after envye, with accusations after infamy, with condemnation after accusations, with iudgement after condemnation, with imprisonment after iudgement, with banishment after imprisonment, for *Simul ista mundi conditor posuit Deus, odium atque regnum.* [A handwritten marginal note construes this as "God which made the world put these two things allwayes together, hatred & government."] But if you shall not countenance them . . . the citizens shall mutinie . . . yea this action of reformation shall fall to the ground, and the common-weale it selfe may not long continue. (Beacon 1594: 91–2)

It seems unlikely, though not impossible, that Grey is the deputy referred to here, judging from the way Beacon represents him when he mentions Grey specifically:

After this maner [after listing examples of punishments which instill fear and thus

> obedience] by a severe discipline of lawes did the *Lorde Gray* in times past, and now *Sir R. Bingehame*, mightily reforme and advance the government of Salamina, so as wee may truely say, by such governours must this nation be reformed. (Beacon 1594: 16)

16 Enuy's relation to snakes is discussed in detail by Jane Aptekar (1969: 202–11).

17 As with the Timias/Amoret episode, Spenser also introduces some ambiguity into Serena's actions. She and Calepine are "much abasht" by Calidore's abrupt entrance in the middle of their "quiet loues delight" (VI.iii.21) – although he is equally embarrassed by his rudeness – and her wounded state makes it difficult for Calepine to perform his chivalrous duties (VI.iii.49). Her wound does not respond to external measures because "it was inwardly vnsound" (VI.iv.16), which could imply that she shares culpability for her infamy. When Calepine gets separated from her in pursuing a quest, she worsens her own case: "And euer more and more her owne affliction wrought" (VI.v.6). However, the point is not, I think, that she is deserving of the Beast's attack, but that she needs to exercise restraint over common human foibles in order to protect herself from the malevolence of slander.

18 Bednarz also sees this attack as an echo of an earlier ambush of Timias by the foresters in III.v, which he reads as an allegory of an ambush Ralegh successfully routed during the Desmond rebellion (Bednarz 1983: 52–7). Grey was Lord Deputy in Ireland during this time and acted ruthlessly to suppress the uprising; Ralegh served as a captain under Grey, participating in the massacre at Smerwick (Bednarz 1983: 56).

19 Paul Alpers suggests the connections between Calidore and the pastoral poets Melibee and Colin Clout; Calidore is also a "surrogate for the reader and the poet" (Alpers 1989: 801). My reading of Book VI has benefited from this article and conversations with its author.

20 Hamilton refers to J. C. Maxwell who remarks that it takes an effort "*not* to identify the hunt after shadowes vaine with the quest which Calidore abandons" (Maxwell 1952: 146). I fail to see why one would need to make this effort.

21 For a discussion of the expression of anti-court sentiment in libels and its connections to political conflict, see Cust (1986, especially 75–9).

22 I would like to thank Janet Adelman for raising the question of why Spenser deflates the allegory in Book IV, and for suggesting his disillusionment with this genre as a project.

23 Bennett argues that this episode was motivated not by "the long-past wrongs of the dead Lord Grey" but by the more recent events surrounding the actions of another of Elizabeth's military commanders, Sir John Norris. Norris had been involved in the struggle to keep the Spanish out of France from 1591 until 1595 when he was called to Ireland to suppress the Tyrone rebellion; Spenser represents these incidents in the Burbon and Irena episodes of cantos xi and xii (Bennett 1942: 193–5, 199–200). The attack by Enuy and Detraction could be read as the response to Norris' failure to establish a secure truce in Ireland. Bennett's evidence that the

Enuy and Detraction episode was added as the poem went to press is persuasive (Bennett 1942: 201–5), and Spenser's admiration for Norris is demonstrated in the dedicatory sonnet to the latter; the tumultuous events in Ireland during the winter of 1595–6 in which Norris figured could certainly account for the poet's anger over criticism of the commander. However, it is clear that while Norris may have provided an occasion for a representation of the attack, he is probably at best a type for Grey, another dedicated public servant abused for the loyal performance of his duty. It is not clear from Bennett's account of the events that Norris was in fact slandered or that Spenser would have known about it. In addition, Norris was not recalled to England before the publication of the *Faerie Queene*, a fact which suggests that the scene of the defamatory attack still might have pointed, at least partially, to Grey's experience.

24 I want to acknowledge the caveat that Jean Brink makes in pointing out that the authorship and the stability of the text of *A View* are still open to question (Brink 1990: 204). My argument does not rest entirely on the *View*, but the strong textual echoes between the neologistic "Blatant Beast" and the "blatter[ing]" of envy in *A View* (Spenser 1934: 27) point to common authorship. See Hotson 1958 for a discussion of the origins of "blatant."

25 We get a sense of this double perspective of Lord Grey's slander later in *A View* during a discussion of his tenure in Ireland in which Irenius argues that English control was subverted through too much leniency. Spenser characterizes the policy of pardoning rebels as a "perillous deuise . . . and verie Cvnningelie contriued, by sowinge first dyssension betwene him [i.e. Grey] and another noble personage, wherein they both at length found, how notablie they had bene abused, and how thereby vnderhand, this vniuersall alteracyon of thinges was brought about, But then to late to staye the same: For in the meane tyme all that was formerlie doen with longe labour and greate toyle was . . . in a moment vndone, and that good Lord blotted with the name of a bloodye man" (Spenser 1934: 137–8). Eudoxus subsequently inquires about the Smerwicke massacre, in which Grey executed those rebels who had given themselves up and asked for mercy. Irenius presents a justification of the Lord Deputy's actions, and concludes: "Therefore most vntrewlie and malyciouslie doe these evill tonges backbyte and slander the sacred ashes of that most iust and honorable personage, whose least vertue of manye most excellent which abounded in his heroicke spirite, they were never able to aspyer vnto" (Spenser 1934: 140). Eudoxus' response reveals the contemporary significance of Grey's reputation:

> I am right gladd to bee thus satisfyed by you in that I haue often heard questyoned, and yett was neuer able till now, to choke the mouth of such detractors with the certain knowledge of theire slanderous vntruths Neither is the knowledge therof impertinent to that which wee formerlie had in hand I meane to the through [*sic*] prosecutinge of that sharpe course which yee haue sett downe, for the bringinge vnder of those Rebells of Vlster and Connaght and preparinge a waye to theire perpetuall reformacion least happelie by any such synister suggestyons of creweltie,

and to much blood shedd all the plott might bee over throwen, and all the cost and Labour therein employed bee vtterlie lost and cast awaye. (Spenser 1934: 140–1)

26 David Norbrook presented the earliest persuasive corrective to this oversight; my argument is deeply indebted to his work. Some other subsequent notable exceptions have been provided by Julia Reinhard Lupton (1987), Rick Rambuss (1993) and Chris Highley (1993).

27 For a discussion, from a different perspective, of Spenser's tenuous relation to the English state, see Brady (1986: 17–18).

28 It should be noted that Spenser's acquisition of Kilcoman castle was a direct result of the suppression of the Desmond rebellion; Ralegh was similarly a beneficiary, receiving a sizable portion of his estate from confiscated properties (Bednarz 1983: 57).

29 This would appear to complete the process of redefining slander in poet–state relations begun in the Proem to Book IV and continued in the depiction of Bon/Malfont. The poet has been transformed from the slanderer of state to the victim of state slander.

30 Thus Spenser's vindication of Grey is motivated by a desire to make acceptable his own, similar, policies, policies that were unacceptable because of their extreme brutality. By obscuring the fact of their cruelty he is able to advocate a program, however horrible, that will finally bring Ireland under submission, all the while maintaining the moral high ground necessary to justify his role of poet advising a prince. Ciaran Brady persuasively argues this point in his analysis of the tensions created in *A View of the Present State of Ireland* by the poet's paradoxical impulses to advocate a cruel policy and yet retain his humanistic claim to virtuous advice:

> Spenser . . . was clearly anxious that his radical argument should be associated with the long tradition of humanist reform thought on Ireland, and made all the more acceptable for that . . . [I]t remained vital to the principal purpose of the poet of the *Faerie Queene* that the English should continue along their path of moral development and not become brutalized by the task which they were being urged to undertake in Ireland. Thus Spenser would make no blunt call for the use of extreme violence; rather it was essential that the good humanist, Eudoxus, should be truly convinced by the man of experience, Irenius, that his was the only way of bringing about the permanent reform of Ireland. (Brady 1986: 47)

By characterizing criticism of the ruthless measures as slander, the moral focus is shifted from condemning brutality to attacking malicious imputations. The refusal to follow the advice offered in *A View* is tantamount to joining in with the defamers of Artegall at the end of Book V.

This is the same move Spenser makes in defending Ralegh in the Timias/Amoret/Belphoebe episode; although Timias is actually guilty (Ralegh did marry Elizabeth Throckmorton against Elizabeth's wishes), he is represented as behaving innocently and the blame is shifted to Belphoebe, who dishonors him in jumping to a "false" conclusion. The allegation of defamation is used to shift attention from the real moral issue at hand by substituting a false one. Thus, Spenser's employment of slander enables him to redefine the crux of a moral dilemma while maintaining the position of a virtuous reformer. This actually results in Spenser fomenting a slander against his critics: by falsely accusing them of slander, he is, in essence, slandering them.

3 SATIRE AND THE ARRAIGNMENT OF THE *POETASTER*

1 O. J. Campbell links the late sixteenth-century rise in political satire with increasing dissatisfaction at Elizabeth granting monopolies and the periodic food shortages (Campbell 1970: 21). Ian Archer argues that conditions in the 1590s might not have been as bad as earlier periods in the sixteenth century, but there is "a strong case for asserting the reality of a *perceived* crisis in the 1590s" (Archer 1991: 14).

2 In the first printing of the play, Jonson of course takes the opportunity to respond to this censure: "At the close of the Quarto text Jonson tells us, with ill-concealed disgust, that the play 'had another Catastrophe or Conclusion, at the first Playing', which, as bringing the Queen upon the stage in person, was by 'many' not relished, and therefore ''twas since alter'd' " (Herford and Simpson 1925–52, III: 374).

3 Herford and Simpson remark on this "Jonsonian attitude" (Herford and Simpson 1925–52, I: 11). Although Jonson did compose numerous epigrams, a related genre banned by the bishops, he did not leave behind any formal verse satires such as those produced in the 1590s. Drummond does mention, however, that Jonson did "read . . . a Satyre [presumably of his own composition?] telling there was no abuses to writte a Satyre of and <in> which he repeateth all the abuses in England and the world" (*Conversations*, Herford and Simpson 1925–52, I: 135).

4 Campbell also notices the connection with the law, commenting that the satirist's "favorite symbols are the instruments of castigation and judicial torture: the scourge, the lash, the rack, the strappado" (Campbell 1970: 35). Andrew Gurr suggests that railing or satirical plays had a strong following among the Inns of Court crowd: "The fashion for railing tried chiefly to appeal to the gallants and law students whose enthusiasm for railing in print was halted by the bishops and their book-burning in 1599. Jonson's transfer of railing to the Shakespeare company's stage [with *Every Man Out*] is one of the pieces of evidence linking them more with gallant and law student playgoers" (Gurr 1987: 155).

5 The distinction between verbal and written defamation and an increasing sense of their danger appear to have developed in the latter half of the sixteenth century. "Statutes of 1554 and 1558 had made it a misdemeanor to speak or write with a malicious intent false and slanderous words of the king or queen. In 1580–81 writing such words was declared to be felony, and speaking such words was declared to be felony on a second conviction" (Holdsworth 1927–66, IV: 511–12).

6 There are notable exceptions; evidence for fear of rumor is found shortly after the arrest of Essex in a February 1601 proclamation "Placing London Vagabonds under Martial Law":

Whereas advertisement is given unto us that there is at this time dispersed within our city of London and the suburbs thereof a great multitude of base and loose people such as neither have any certain place of abode nor any good or lawful cause of business to attend hereabouts, but lie privily in corners and bad houses, listening after news and stirs, and spreading rumors and tales, being of likelihood ready to lay hold of any occasion to enter into any tumult or disorder, thereby to seek rapine and pillage . . .

Therefore we do straightly command and charge all persons that such loose people having no certain dwelling or abode within the city and suburbs thereof, or otherwise no sufficient cause to stay or lawful business, presently avoid and get them down into the country; upon pain of death by martial law to be executed upon them. (Hughes and Larkin 1964–9, III: 232–3)

The severity of this decree is no doubt due to the uneasy state of affairs in London after the failed uprising.

7 Ferdinando Pulton comments on the difference between the public threat of "menacer" and the anonymous attack of the "libeller":

The menacer layeth open his name, and his griefe, and standeth in the face of his enemie, and discouereth the corasiue of his mind, and dothe thereby giue a forewarning to his aduersarie to prouide for, and defend himselfe: But this secret canker the libeller, concealeth his name, hideth himselfe in a corner, & priuily stingeth him in fame, reputation, & credit, who then neither knoweth from whom, or vpon what cause he receiueth his blowes, nor yet hath meanes therein to defend himselfe. (Pulton 1609: B^{v})

S.F.C. Milsom speculates on the reasoning behind the notion that written defamation poses a greater threat than spoken:

Since, as the star chamber itself concluded, the mischiefs of the offence could lie as much in speech as in writing, the early preoccupation with writing must have had a deeper cause than the chronic governmental dislike of the printing press. The only trace of a reason given by Coke is an analogy with poisoning: harm easily done in secret must be severely punished when brought to light. (Milsom 1981: 389–90)

8 While Jonson was jailed, questioned or forced to revise his texts because of perceived political threats in several plays, recent criticism suggests that dramatic criticism was not understood to be as dangerous to the state as printed works of non-fiction, such as histories or political commentary. Philip Finkelpearl demonstrates that a great deal of criticism against the ruler could and did get past an inefficient Master of the Revels. Richard Burt advances a similar and more nuanced account of the dynamics of state licensing and stage license (Burt 1993: 78–114). Leeds Barroll cautions critics against assuming that the state's concerns with texts related to the Essex rebellion were directed equally toward the dramatized history and printed history: "the Privy Council showed in its responses more concern for the danger represented by Hayward's book [on Henry IV] than for that occasioned by Shakespeare's drama . . . One could argue, in fact, that the Elizabethan authorities perceived in connection with the Essex plot a threat much more serious than acted plays: i.e., the printed book" (Barroll 1988: 452). The severest punishments for verbal attacks of state practice,

the mutilations of Stubbes and Prynne, both resulted from printed texts, not spoken plays.

9 All citations of Jonson's works are from Herford and Simpson (1925–52).

10 I follow what I perceive to be Jonson's lead here in conflating poetry and drama in my discussion of *Poetaster*. Generally, with regard to the "comicall satires," Jonson has done so himself in transferring satire from the page to the stage. However, he also aligns poetry and drama specifically in this play; the author of *Poetaster* is menaced by Envy in the Induction, as Ovid is harassed by embodiments of envy delineated in his elegy. While the champions of poetry in Augustan Rome are poets, as distinguished from scurrilous players, Jonson, the playwright, identifies himself (though disingenuously disclaiming the comparison) with the former in the "Apologetical Dialogue" (98–107). Although Jonson often disparages the stage in the prologues to his plays and his poetry he did not, I believe, see drama as a genre inherently inferior to poetry. He condemned only those plays (and the audiences who enjoyed them) written by inferior practitioners, as he obviously thought highly of his own dramatic endeavors. Ernest William Talbert comments on Jonson's equation of play with poem: "One of the best illustrations of the fact that a play was considered a poem is Jonson's dedication of *Volpone* to the two Universities 'for their love and acceptance shew'n to his poeme in the presentation'" (Talbert 1945: 233, note 34). Jonas Barish presents a thoughtful commentary on Jonson's preference for print versus performance, which suggests that he was anxious that the drama be taken as poetry: "Jonson is not interested in vindicating his plays as theater, but in validating them as literature, as dramatic poems" (Barish 1981: 139).

11 I concur with the opinion of Herford and Simpson that the elegy Ovid speaks in the play is based on Marlowe's translation of the *Amores*, I.xv (Herford and Simpson 1925–52: 538, note to I.i.43–84). However, Jonson emends Marlowe's version considerably, leaving only four of the forty-one lines of the poem unchanged. Jonson's version was printed after Marlowe's in the second edition of the *Amores*, suggesting that while they are different enough to be published as two separate versions, they were nevertheless connected in the mind of the printer and, presumably, in the minds of his reading public. Thanks to Joel Altman who brought to my attention the fact that Jonson included in his play a version of the banned Marlowe translation.

12 Richard McCabe argues that, in spite of the alleged pornographic content of some of the prohibited works, the target of the ban was satire and the primary motivation political, not moral. He reproduces the text of the Ban and describes the implementation of the order (McCabe 1981: 189, 190–1).

13 Many critics have discussed the play in terms of a defense of poetry. Most notable in setting forth the argument that Jonson is defending Ovid, as well as Virgil and Horace, from attacks on poets and poetry are Talbert (1945), and Norbert Platz (1973).

14 "The last act of *Poetaster* is supplementary to the plot of the comedy. That business is over with in the fourth act. So is the social satire which establishes the tone of the drama. However, the catastrophe of Ovid and

his associates must be shared by all their hangers-on, including the poetasters. They are soiled by the guilt of the morally disruptive tendencies of the courtly group and must also be punished" (Campbell 1970: 131–2).

15 Katherine Maus strikes a balance between those critics who condemn Ovid, on the one hand, and those who champion him, on the other, "Ovid is neither the exemplar of the good life nor a serious social threat, neither poetaster nor true poet. In the Augustan world of *Poetaster*, Ovid is socially marginal; Jonson's audience, conditioned by erotic comedy, has trouble with him because it fails to recognize a red herring when it sees one . . . Jonson quite literally banishes Ovid from his play after a parodic balcony scene with Julia, and with him disappear all vestiges of romance. What supersedes it is the more typically Jonsonian process of exposure and purgation, a ritual overseen by the public poets Horace and Virgil, and sponsored by the authority of an emperor. This drama, and not the drama of frustrated love, produces the regenerated comic society of the conclusion" (Maus 1984: 91–2).

16 *The Metamorphosis of Pigmalions Image and Certain Satires* and *The Scourge of Villanie* are both included on the list of prohibited works (McCabe 1981: 188, 191).

17 Waith makes this point with regard to the character of Ovid: "If the good poet must be a good man, it is understandable that a defense of poetry should present the case of the morally irresponsible poet, in order to show that he is not reckoned among the good. By publicly disowning the reprobate, the other poets dissociate themselves from the scandal of his behavior and thus defend themselves against the charge of wantonness so frequently made by the detractors of poetry" (Waith 1951: 15).

18 Act IV.vi.30–59. Augustus initially addresses this speech to the "parcell-*poet*" Crispinus, but as he continues it is clear by his use of plural nouns – "When you . . . / Liue, as [virtue] were no law vnto your liues" – that he is addressing all the poets. The emperor's specific punishment of Ovid suggests that he holds the love poet most at fault for failing to teach virtue. He accuses Ovid of "soothing the declin'd affections / Of our base daughter" – promoting vice rather than performing his didactic task. Love poetry was often accused in the early modern period of leading to debauchery, as I have noted earlier in my discussion of the Proem to Book IV of *The Faerie Queene*.

19 Platz discusses Jonson's use of *laudando praecipere* and the poet's role in the state as quoted in the *Discoveries* (Platz 1973: 20). Joseph John Kelly points out that Jonson's independent stance with regard to the ruler is played out in *Poetaster*:

> Jonson's inability to whitewash Augustus even in a comedy where he is primarily a royal patron, not the emperor, along with his treatment of Horace and Vergil as Caesar's equals, suggests that Jonson-Horace was a very independent royalist. He wanted to be a licensed satirist like the Horace of *Poetaster*, he valued a monarchy that established peace after civil war and promoted the arts, but he remained suspicious of royal power and fantasized that the Horaces and Vergils of his day would effectively rule the realm through their counsel. (Kelly 1983: 204)

Kelly refers to Jonson's comment in the *Discoveries* that Augustus' respect for Horace moved the ruler to offer him a position in the state:

> [Horace was] a man so gratious, and in high favour with the Emperour, as *Augustus* often called him his wittie *Manling*, (for the littlenes of his stature;) and (if wee may trust Antiquity) had design'd him for a Secretary of Estate; and invited him to the P<a>lace, which he modestly praid off, and refus'd. (Herford and Simpson 1925–52, VIII: 643)

20 While the harshest attacks on the law do not appear in the Quarto text, Herford and Simpson believe that they did exist in the original script and were re-introduced, and not newly written, in the 1616 Folio. "It is significant that two insertions of the Folio strengthen the satire on lawyers and players, two classes who protested strongly against the treatment of their order in the original text . . . It is probable that this passage, like the 'Apologetical Dialogue', gave trouble – as well it might – was judiciously cancelled in the Quarto, and revived in the Folio" (Herford and Simpson 1925–52, IV: 193). It seems unlikely that the lawyers would have complained about the play in the absence of these passages.

21 Herford and Simpson suggest that the introduction "of a great Roman lawyer, who was broad-minded enough to be on friendly terms with a Roman satirist" was intended "to silence legal carpers in London" (Herford and Simpson 1925–52, IV: 194).

22 The contemporary definition of slander as a tort was more or less in agreement with Trebatius; truth was an allowable defense among private persons in a slander case tried in a common law court. However, the valid accusations of "persons of good qualitie" which Horace shuns in III.v.131 would constitute defamation under the *scandalum magnatum* statute. Furthermore, under the laws of libel as enforced by the Star Chamber, the truth was not a defense, and defamations of public persons were considered a greater offense, because more likely to result in a breach of the peace (Coke 1907: 251).

23 Herford and Simpson give a brief account of the custom in their introduction to *Poetaster*: "From a very early time the felicitous aptness of the historical Vergil's speech, its wealth of unsuspected relevance, its mysterious depth and pregnancy, the large humanity even of its 'lonely words', were implicitly recognized by the custom of resorting to his volume for guidance at every 'serious' point. The practice of Sortes Virgilianae was current in England until long after Jonson's time, and it is quite likely that he had it directly in mind" (Herford and Simpson 1925–52, I: 436). They cite an instance in which "Charles I and Falkland consulted the Virgilian oracle in the Bodleian, turning up *Aen.* iv. 615" (Herford and Simpson 1925–52, I: 436, note 1).

24 The historical Ovid's depiction of Dido in *Heroides* VII is arguably more sympathetic to her plight than Virgil's, thus lending further support to Jonson's distinction between poetry of love and poetry of virtue.

25 A false accusation of felony constituted slander, because it "endangered the life or liberty of the plaintiff, for instance by arrest and trial" (Baker 1990: 498). Coke discusses libelous pictures in the case *de Libellis Famosis*:

"*Famosus libellus sine scriptis* may be, 1. *Picturis*, as to paint the party in any shameful and ignominious manner. 2. *Signis*, as to fix a gallows, or other reproachful and ignominious signs at the party's door or elsewhere" (Coke 1907: 251–2). William Hudson also touches on the matter of libellous pictures: "Picturing or setting up horns at a man's gate was severely punished in the Case of *Horsey* v. *Astley* 33. & 34. *Eliz*. And in the great libel of *Wells*, there being a fame against a townsman that he lived incontinently with the wife of the plaintiff *Hole*, in a May-game used yearly in that town they brought a man riding with a board before him on which was a pair of nine-holes, one riding at the one side saying, *He holes for a groat*; the defendants being many in number were severely punished for this pastime" (Hudson 1791–2, II:101). Caesar's pronouncement that a signed document could not be a libel (V.iii.55–6) was a common misconception in the early modern period, according to Hudson (1791–2, II:102). Written language which resulted in a breach of the peace, signed or unsigned, still constituted libel.

26 Caesar requests that Virgil keep his seat when the accusers first break in (V.iii.27).

27 Ernest Talbert notices that Lupus' punishment for disturbing the emperor's peace, being fit with a pair of "larger ears" (V.iii.129–33), is reminiscent of the famous and often reproduced painting, *The Judgement of Apelles*, in which a ruler listening to slander is depicted with large ears. The original painting was lost before the early modern period, but a description survived in Lucian's treatise on slander. This account of the image inspired many artists to portray the scene, most notably Botticelli and Dürer. Talbert cites Thomas Elyot's discussion in *The Book Named the Governor* of Apelles' image:

> Whiche in myn oppinion is a right necessary mater to be in tables or hangynges set in euery mans house that is in auctoritee. For in good faythe to gyue place to detraction at the begynnynge, it is a thinge childisshe and base, and to be estemed amonge the moost great inconueniences and mischiefes. These be well nyghe the wordes of Luciane; whether the counsayle be good I remitte it to the wise redars. Of one thing I am sure, that *by detraction as well many good wittes haue bene drowned, as also vertue, and paynfull study haue (bene) unrewarded, and many zelatours or fauourers of the publyke weale haue benne discouraged.* (in Talbert 1945: 248)

Elyot also brings up the question of credulity and interpretation in this passage, both in warning his readers to avoid believing slanders, and in exhorting them to be wise in their judgment of Lucian's words. Jonson shows his idealized ruler to be immune to the trains of detraction, but exposes a lesser public official to ridicule for attending to slanders.

28 This statement offers opposing interpretations: either that Horace is the least capable accuser there is, or that he is the most guilty of making accusations. I will discuss the ways in which Jonson's defensive attack turns back against him in my examination of the "Apologetical Dialogue" later in this chapter.

29 PRO STAC 8 5/18. I have provided punctuation where it is needed and have silently expanded contractions; otherwise, I have retained the spelling of the bill.

30 Herford and Simpson assume, I think correctly, that Tucca had voted not guilty, and later tried to change his vote to avoid appearing connected with the clearly guilty defendants. They interpret "Parcell-guiltie" as *non liquet*, or "not proven."

31 Herford and Simpson assume that Virgil is probably simply the historical Virgil, and dismiss the notion that the epic poet is meant to represent any contemporary poet (Herford and Simpson 1925–52, I: 432–7).

32 Penniman makes this claim in the introduction of his edition of Jonson's *Poetaster* and Dekker's *Satiromastix* (1913). To my knowledge, no official record exists indicating that Jonson was brought before the Lord Chief Justice. This assertion may, however, be inferred from the dedication of *Poetaster* to Martin, who is there described as "a noble and timely vndertaker, to the greatest Iustice of this kingdome" (lines 11–12). Herford and Simpson gloss "the greatest Iustice" as "Sir John Popham, lord chief justice from 1592 to his death in 1607" (Herford and Simpson 1925–52, IX: 534). They do not suggest that Jonson was actually brought before Popham, however. Although Penniman's conjecture cannot be considered authoritative, the fact that Jonson did not print the dedication in the Quarto, as he might logically have done to thank his friend after a close scrape, could indicate, as the suppression of the "Apologetical Dialogue" suggests, that things were still too controversial to make any reference to the author's troubles.

33 I do not consider the scene between Horace and Trebatius in the discussion that follows, even though it adds interesting dimensions to Jonson's defense of satire, because it was not included in the play until the 1616 Folio, and thus is irrelevant to the events surrounding the response to the first appearance of the play and the author's immediate attempts to quell his critics in the "Apologetical Dialogue." Because the address to the reader in the 1616 Folio specifically refers to these events in its introduction to the "Apologetical Dialogue" I include it in my analysis.

34 Most commentators on the War of the Theaters argue that characters in *Every Man Out* and *Cynthia's Revels* are also intended, although less explicitly, to represent Marston and Dekker, so Jonson's claims to have forborne the attacks of his critics until the presentation of *Poetaster* should be seen as disingenuous at best. For a thorough exploration of the "poets' war" see Bednarz (1991).

35 I'm grateful to Tom Garrity for bringing to my attention Aristotle's identification of the iamb as the appropriate foot for satire and invective in the *Poetics* (IV.10); it is tantalizing to speculate how this relates to the fact that the iambic pentameter was the meter used most commonly in early modern drama and poetry.

36 Although Jonson escaped execution for the murder of Gabriel Spencer by claiming benefit of clergy, he was nevertheless punished with "confiscation of all his goods, and the Tyburn brand on his thumb" (Herford and Simpson 1925–52, I: 18–19).

37 Baumlin (1986) discusses the satirist's self-incrimination in Donne's hand-

ling of Horace's *Sermon* I.9, the same satire Jonson uses in III.i in the scene with Crispinus. He comments that this self-deprecation, while made more explicit in Donne's presentation of the scene, is nevertheless extant in the original. I would suggest that Jonson attempted to suppress this aspect of Horace's poetry, so as to present a seamless defense of satire, only to have it re-emerge in the self-defense of his "Apologetical Dialogue."

38 This point is most clearly demonstrated in Horace's response to Lupus' accusation:

> A iust man cannot feare, thou foolish *Tribune*;
> Not, though the malice of traducing tongues,
> The open vastnesse of a tyrannes eare,
> The senselesse rigour of the wrested lawes,
> Or the red eyes of strain'd authoritie
> Should, in a point, meet all to take his life.
> His innocence is armour 'gainst all these. (v.iii.61–7)

4 SLANDER FOR SLANDER IN *MEASURE FOR MEASURE*

1 I want to make clear here that I am focusing in this chapter on a specific and limited area of slander within the works of Shakespeare. For the purposes of this book, I am mainly concerned with his representation of slander in the context of the conflict between poet and ruler; however, this hardly exhausts the range of his representations of defamation. The problems slander poses in the second tetralogy, while political, are not the same ones explored in *Measure for Measure*; the *Sonnets* engage in the dynamics of detraction in another different context, as does *Hamlet*, as do the plays representing slanders against women: *Much Ado*, *Othello*, *Winter's Tale*, and *Cymbeline*. For treatments of these various other aspects of infamy, see Boose (1995), Gowing (1993), Gross (1989), Jardine (1991), Kaplan and Eggert (1996) and Sexton (1978).

2 There is evidence in the records of sixteenth-century Essex that "unfavorable or irreverent remarks about the sovereign," such as accusing the queen of being a whore or of bearing and murdering illegitimate children, received very harsh penalties, even though such comments did not directly incite to rebellion (Samaha 1975: 70).

3 Reginald Lawson sees Lucio as behaving "according to the 'trick' or fashion of his group. A fantastic is defined variously by Elizabethans as 'an improvident young gallant'; 'an effeminate fool'; . . . 'and one that is so neere a kin to the foole, that they cannot marry without a license from the Pope'" (Lawson 1937: 262). Mary Lascelles claims that this epithet for Lucio should not be attributed to Shakespeare:

> The Folio attaches lists of Actors' (i.e. characters') names to seven plays. Mr. Crompton Rhodes supposes them to derive from papers which served some useful purpose in the theatre, as "a remembrancer for casting, or as a catalogue to a bundle of written parts." (*Shakespeare's First Folio*, Oxford, 1923, p. 118.) This supposition as to their provenance does not necessarily connect them with the dramatist, and the

list for *Measure for Measure* contains one word to which there is no Shakespearian parallel. Lucio is called "a fantastique" – meaning, presumably, a fop. Shakespeare uses the adjective fantastic in a corresponding sense: "To be fantastic may become a youth" (*Two Gentlemen*, II.vii.47); but his form for the noun is fantastico: "such antic, lisping, affecting fantasticoes" (*Romeo and Juliet*, II.iv.30). I believe that we should not associate this list with him, nor build on it any surmise as to the form in which he found his plot, or left his play. (Lascelles 1953: 165)

Ms. Lascelles is probably justified in her assumption that Shakespeare would have used the term "fantastico" to indicate a simpering gallant. However, I do not see either Lucio or the Duke, who is described as "fantastical" in the course of the play, as a fop. I wish to suggest another definition of fantastic that would have been available to Shakespeare, one which applies to both the Duke and Lucio and that, regardless of the authenticity of the *dramatis personae*, is supported by the text of the play. J. M. Nosworthy's comment on Lucio's designation as a "fantastic" in his edition of *Measure for Measure* suggests the direction my argument will take: "The word may imply a fop, but in Lucio's case it seems more likely to signify someone with an unbridled fantasy or imagination" (Shakespeare 1969: 154).

4 One intriguing appearance of the fantastic should at least be mentioned here, although its relevance to *Measure for Measure* is tenuous. Related to legislation punishing witchcraft and the invocation of evil spirits (which laws enjoyed a renaissance during the early years of James I's reign) were the mid-sixteenth-century statutes directed against false and fantastical prophecies. "The making of such prophecies was declared to be felony in 1541–42; and after the repeal of this statute in 1547 such prophecies were made misdemeanors by statutes of 1549 and 1562–3. The reason for the enactment of these two latter statutes, and probably of the first-named also, was the fact that these prophecies were made for the purpose of stirring up rebellion" (Holdsworth 1927–66, IV: 511). A later statute on the containment of masterless men (39 Eliz. 4) classed as vagabonds anyone "using any subtile Crafte or unlawful Games and Playes, or fayning themselves to have knowledge in Phisiognomye, Palmestry or other like crafty Scyence, or pretending that they can tell Destenyes Fortunes or such other like fantastical Imagyna[c]ons; . . . all Fencers Bearewards co[m]on Players of Enterludes and Minstrells wandring abroade (other then Players of Enterludes belonging to any Baron of this realme . . .)."

5 Little is known about Mazzoni's reception in England before Milton. I include Mazzoni in this discussion to indicate that contemporary literary theory was developing a specific definition of the fantastic. Puttenham's similar account suggests either that he had read Mazzoni, or that this understanding of the word was already circulating amongst literary theorists in sixteenth-century England.

6 See Lawry for the suggestion that Lucio functions as director in II.ii (Lawry 1982: 225).

7 Summarized in Spencer (1965: 17–18). He argues that the text does not

provide a motivation for Lucio's actions towards the Duke if he did know the latter was in disguise. I would agree with him in part, but this does not nullify the fact that Lucio does speak the truth here. Shakespeare may be playing with the notion of "fantastic" as it related to such supernatural knowledge as predicting the future (see note 4). At any rate, my analysis of his character focuses on his function in the play with regard to the Duke, so I tend to concentrate on the etymological, rather than psychological, significance of his behavior.

8 Insulting language about a magistrate was considered defamatory because it posed a threat to the peace of the realm by calling into question the ruler's judgment. As Edward Coke states in *de Libellis Famosis*, "what greater scandal of Government can there be than to have corrupt or wicked magistrates to be appointed and constituted by the King to govern his subjects under him?" (Coke 1907: 251). I will discuss at a later point and in greater detail the significance of this theory for the Duke's actions.

9 Pauline Croft's analysis of libels representing sexual promiscuity suggests it is a trope for political corruption (Croft 1991: 59–60). G. K. Hunter (1973) makes a similar point about sexual corruption hinting at political corruption in the genre of tragi-comedies such as *Measure for Measure*.

10 Jonson's depiction of Fame is a translation of Virgil's description of Fama in *Aeneid* iv: 181–3.

> monstrum horrendum, ingens, cui quot sunt corpore plumae, tot vigilies oculi subter (mirabile dictu), tot linguae, totidem ora sonant, tot subrigit auris.

> a horrible, huge monster, whose body was covered with as many feathers as vigilant eyes underneath (miraculous to tell), as many tongues, again as many sounding mouths, as many attentive ears.

Depictions of Fame often showed her covered with sense organs; the "Rainbow portrait" of Elizabeth (*c.* 1600) represents her in a dress embroidered with ears and eyes, symbolizing Fame (Strong 1963: 84–5, plate xvii). In the stage direction to the Induction of *2 Henry IV*, Rumour enters "painted full of tongues."

11 Escalus' name might be derived from "scale" with roots in the German word for "balance." It is probably more closely linked to the Latin *scala*, indicating "staircase, ladder, standard of measurement." The Latin root is also related to *scandere*, "to climb," and thus to such words as "ascend" and "scandal." The Duke would not have "measured up" to Escalus' superior leadership, which would have resulted in a scandal for the ruler.

12 See Bawcutt (1984) for a discussion of the Duke's condemnation of Angelo on the basis of the latter's hypocrisy. Although I disagree with the article's sympathetic attitude toward the Duke, I find its account of where he finds fault with Angelo particularly convincing.

13 Lucio's apparent ability to "see through" the Duke is emphasized in the language as well as the action of this moment:

> You must be hooded
> must you? Show your knave's visage, with a

pox to you! Show your sheep-biting face, and be
hanged an hour! Will't not off? (v.i.350–3)

The Arden note on "sheep-biting face" (352) suggests there is a grain of truth in the midst of this fantastical formulation: " 'sheep-biter', i.e. a dog or wolf that attacked sheep, was a common epithet for a dangerous rogue, especially a sanctimonious one." In his ostensible attempts to defend his state from the dangers of slander, Vincentio actually poses a greater threat to order in the realm.

CONCLUSION

1 For related essays on the circulation of public opinion and libels see Cogswell (1990), Croft (1991), Cust (1986), and Fox (1994). Interestingly, while these works, including Bellany's (1993), often consider literary connections to libels, they largely ignore or misunderstand the substantial legal history on defamation that circumscribes their discussions.

Works cited

Alpers, Paul 1989, "Spenser's Late Pastorals," *ELH* 56(4): 797–817.

American Heritage Dictionary of Indo-European Roots 1985, Calvert Watkins (ed.) Boston: Houghton-Mifflin.

Aptekar, Jane 1969, *Icons of Justice: Iconography and Thematic Imagery in Book V of "The Faerie Queene"*, New York: Columbia University Press.

Archer, Ian 1991, *The Pursuit of Stability: Social Relations in Elizabethan London*, Cambridge University Press.

Bagwell, Richard 1890, *Ireland Under the Tudors*, vol. III. London: Longmans, Green & Co.

Baker, J. H. 1979, *An Introduction to English Legal History*, 2nd edn. London: Butterworths.

1990, *An Introduction to English Legal History*, 3rd edn. London: Butterworths.

Baker, J. H., and Milsom, S. F. C. 1986, *Sources of English Legal History*, London: Butterworths.

Barish, Jonas 1981, *The Antitheatrical Prejudice*, Berkeley: University of California Press.

Barroll, Leeds 1988, "A New History for Shakespeare and his Time," *Shakespeare Quarterly* 39: 441–64.

Baumlin, James 1986, "Generic Contexts of Elizabethan Satire: Rhetoric, Poetic Theory, and Imitation," in Barbara Lewalski (ed.) *Renaissance Genres: Essays on Theory, History and Interpretation*, Cambridge: Harvard University Press, pp. 444–67.

Bawcutt, N. W. 1984, "'He who the sword of heaven will bear': The Duke versus Angelo in *Measure for Measure*," *Shakespeare Survey* 37: 89–97.

Beacon, Richard 1594, *Solon his follie, or A Politique Discovrse, Tovching the Reformation of common-weales conquered, declined or corrupted*, Oxford.

Bednarz, James 1983, "Ralegh in Spenser's Historical Allegory," *Spenser Studies* 4: 49–70.

1991, "Representing Jonson: *Histriomastix* and the Origin of the Poets' War," *Huntington Library Quarterly* 54(1): 1–30.

Bellany, Alastair 1993, "'Rayling Rymes and Vaunting Verse': Libellous Politics in Early Stuart England, 1603–1628," in Kevin Sharpe and Peter Lake (eds.) *Culture and Politics in Early Stuart England*, Stanford University Press, pp. 285–310.

Bennett, Josephine 1942, *The Evolution of "The Faerie Queene"*, University of Chicago Press.
Berger, Adolf 1953, *Encyclopedic Dictionary of Roman Law*, Philadelphia: Transactions of the American Philosophical Society, ns, vol. 43.
Boose, Lynda 1995, "The Priest, the Slanderer, the Historia and the Feminist," *English Literary Renaissance* 25(2): 320–40.
Bowen, Catherine Drinker 1956, *The Lion and the Throne*, Boston: Atlantic-Little, Brown.
Bradshaw, Brendan 1988, "Robe and Sword in the Conquest of Ireland," in Claire Cross, David Loades and J.J. Scarisbrick (eds.) *Law and Government under the Tudors*, Cambridge University Press, pp. 139–62.
Brady, Ciaran 1986, "Spenser's Irish Crisis: Humanism and Experience in the 1590s," *Past and Present* 111: 17–49.
Brady, Ciaran and Canny, Nicholas 1988, "Spenser's Irish Crisis: Humanism and Experience in the 1590s," *Past and Present* 120: 201–15.
Brink, Jean 1990, "Constructing the *View of the Present State of Ireland*," *Spenser Studies* 11: 203–28.
Burt, Richard 1993, *Licensed by Authority*, Ithaca: Cornell University Press.
1988, "' 'Tis Writ by Me': Massinger's *The Roman Actor* and the Politics of Reception in the English Renaissance Theatre," *Theatre Journal* 40: 332–46.
Campbell, O. J. 1970, *"Comicall Satyre" and Shakespeare's "Troilus and Cressida"*, San Marino, CA: Henry G. Huntington Library.
Canny, Nicholas 1983, "Edmund Spenser and the Development of an Anglo-Irish Identity," *Yearbook of English Studies* 13: 1–19.
Chambers, E. K. 1923, *The Elizabethan Stage*, 4 vols., Oxford: Clarendon.
Clare, Janet 1990, *Art Made Tongue-tied by Authority*, Manchester University Press.
Cogswell, Thomas 1990, "The Politics of Propaganda: Charles I and the People in the 1620s," *Journal of British Studies* 29(3): 187–215.
Coke, Edward 1907, "de Libellis Famosis," *Reports*, Book 5 in Max A. Robertson and Geoffrey Ellis (eds.) *The English Reports*, King's Bench Division, Book VI. Edinburgh: William Green, vol. 77, pp. 250–2.
Croft, Pauline 1991, "The Reputation of Robert Cecil: Libels, Political Opinion and Popular Awareness in the Early Seventeenth Century," London, *Transactions of the Royal Historical Society*, sixth series, vol. 1, pp. 43–69.
Cunningham, Karen 1992, "'A Spanish heart in an English body': the Ralegh Treason Trial and the Poetics of Proof," *Journal of Medieval and Renaissance Studies* 22(3): 327–51.
Cust, Richard 1986, "News and Politics in Early Seventeenth-Century England," *Past and Present* 112: 60–90.
de Man, Paul 1979, *Allegories of Reading*, New Haven: Yale University Press.
Dutton, Richard 1991, *Mastering the Revels: The Regulation and Censorship of English Renaissance Drama*, University of Iowa Press.
Egerton, Sir P. de M. Grey, ed. 1847, *A Commentary on the Services and*

Charges of William Lord Grey of Wilton, by His Son Arthur, Lord Grey of Wilton. With a Memoir of the Author and Illustrative Documents, London: Camden Society.

Emmison, F. G. 1970, *Elizabethan Life: Disorder*, Essex: Cullingford & Co. Ltd.

Finkelpearl, Philip 1986, "'The Comedians' Liberty': Censorship of the Jacobean Stage Reconsidered," *English Literary Renaissance* 16: 123–39.

Fletcher, Angus 1964, *Allegory: The Theory of a Symbolic Mode*, Ithaca: Cornell University Press.

Fletcher, Anthony 1985, "Honour, Reputation and Local Officeholding in Elizabethan and Stuart England," in Anthony Fletcher and John Stevenson (eds.) *Order and Disorder in Early Modern England*, Cambridge University Press, pp. 92–115.

Foucault, Michel 1979, *Discipline and Punish*. Trans. Alan Sheridan, New York: Vintage.

Fox, Adam 1994, "Ballads, Libels and Popular Ridicule in Jacobean England," *Past and Present* 145: 47–83.

Foxe, John 1870, *Actes and Monuments*, ed. George Townsend, 3rd edn. 8 vols., London.

Goldberg, Jonathan 1981, *Endlesse Werke*, Baltimore: The Johns Hopkins University Press.

1983, *James I and the Politics of Literature*. Baltimore: The Johns Hopkins University Press.

Goodman, Godfrey 1839, *The Court of King James the First*, ed. John S. Brewer, vol. II, London: Richard Bentley.

Gowing, Laura 1993, "Gender and the Language of Insult in Early Modern London," *History Workshop Journal* 35: 1–21.

Grande Dizionario della Lingua Italiana, 1975, Turin: Unione Tipografico-Editrice Torinese.

Greenblatt, Stephen 1973, *Sir Walter Ralegh: The Renaissance Man and His Roles*, New Haven: Yale University Press.

Gross, Kenneth 1989, "Slander and Skepticism in *Othello*," *ELH* 56(4): 819–852.

Gurr, Andrew 1987, *Playgoing in Shakespeare's London*, Cambridge University Press.

Hamilton, A. C., see Spenser, Edmund

Hanson, Elizabeth 1991, "Torture and Truth in Renaissance England," *Representations* 33: 53–84.

Harding, Alan 1973, *A Social History of English Law*. Gloucester, MA: Peter Smith.

Hawarde, John 1894, *Les reportes del cases in Camera Stellata, 1593–1609*, ed. William Paley Baildon. Privately printed.

Helmholz, R. H., ed. 1985, *Select Cases on Defamation to 1600*, vol. 101 of *The Selden Society*, 104 vols to date, London: Publications of the Selden Society, 1887– .

Herford, C. H. and Simpson, Percy and Evelyn eds. 1925–52, *Ben Jonson*, 11 vols., Oxford: Clarendon Press.

Highley, Christopher 1993, "Spenser and the Bards," unpublished paper delivered at the Spenser at Kalamazoo conference, Western Michigan University.

Holdsworth, W. S. 1927–66, *A History of the English Law*, 16 vols. Boston: Little, Brown–Methuen.

Hotson, Leslie 1958, "The Blatant Beast," in Don Cameron Allen (ed.), *Studies in Honor of T. W. Baldwin*, Urbana: University of Illinois Press, pp. 34–7.

Hudson, William 1791–2, *A Treatise of the Court of Star Chamber*, in Francis Hargrave (ed.) *Collectanea Juridica*, 2 vols. London, vol. II.

Hughes, Paul and Larkin, James (eds.), 1964–9, *Tudor Royal Proclamations*, 3 vols., New Haven: Yale University Press.

Hunter, G. K. 1973, "Italian Tragicomedy on the English Stage," *Renaissance Drama* ns VI: 123–48.

Ingram, Martin 1987, *Church Courts, Sex and Marriage in England, 1570–1640*, Cambridge University Press.

James I 1918, *Basilikon Doron*. in Charles McIlwain (ed.) *The Political Works of James I*, Cambridge: Harvard University Press, pp. 3–52.

Jardine, David 1847, *Criminal Trials*, vol. II, London: M.A. Nattali.

Jardine, Lisa 1991, "'Why should he call her whore?' Defamation and Desdemona's Case," in Margaret Tudeau-Clayton and Martin Warner, (eds.) *Addressing Frank Kermode*, Urbana: University of Illinois Press, pp. 124–153.

Jenkins, Raymond 1937, "Spenser with Lord Grey in Ireland," *PMLA* 52 (2): 338–53.

Jones, Robert 1967, "The Satirist's Retirement in Jonson's 'Apologetical Dialogue'," *ELH* 34: 447–67.

Kaplan, M. Lindsay and Eggert, Katherine 1996, "'Good queen, my lord, good queen": Sexual Slander and the Trials of Authority in *The Winter's Tale*," *Renaissance Drama* ns 25: 89–118.

Kelly, Joseph John 1983, "Ben Jonson's Politics," *Renaissance and Reformation* ns 7: 192–215.

Lambert, Sheila 1987, "The Printers and the Government, 1604–1637," in Robin Myers and Michael Harris (eds.) *Aspects of Printing from 1600*, Oxford Polytechnic Press, pp. 1–29.

Lascelles, Mary 1953, *Shakespeare's "Measure for Measure"*, Folcroft, PA: Folcroft.

Lawry, J. S. 1982, "Imitations and Creations in *Measure for Measure*," in Cecile Cary and Henry Limouze (eds.) *Shakespeare and the Arts*, Washington, DC: University Press of America, pp. 217–29.

Lawson, Reginald 1937, "Lucio, in *Measure for Measure*." *English Studies* 29: 259–64.

Lewis, C. T. 1977, *Elementary Latin Dictionary*, Oxford: Clarendon Press.

Loades, David 1991, *Politics, Censorship and the English Reformation*, London and New York: Pinter Publishers.

Loewenstein, Joseph 1984, *Responsive Readings: Versions of Echo in Pastoral, Epic and the Jonsonian Masque*, New Haven: Yale University Press.

Lupton, Julia Reinhard 1987, "Home-Making in Ireland: Virgil's Eclogue I and Book VI of *The Faerie Queene*," *Spenser Studies* 8: 119–45

McCabe, Richard 1981, "Elizabethan Satire and the Bishop's Ban of 1599," *Yearbook of English Studies* 11: 188–93.

Maclean, Ian 1992, *Interpretation and Meaning in the Renaissance: The Case of Law*, Cambridge University Press.

Manning, Roger 1980, "The Origins of the Doctrine of Sedition," *Albion* 12(2): 99–121.

March, John 1647, *Actions for Slander*, London.

Maus, Katherine 1984, *Ben Jonson and the Roman Frame of Mind*, Princeton University Press.

Maxwell, J. C. 1952, "The Truancy of Calidore," *ELH* 19: 143–9.

Mazzoni, Jacopo 1940, 1962, "On the Defense of the *Comedy* of Dante," in Alan Gilbert (ed.) *Literary Criticism: Plato to Dryden* Detroit: Wayne State, pp. 359–403.

Milsom, S. F. C. 1981, *Historical Foundations of the Common Law*, London: Butterworths.

Neale, J. E. 1957, *Queen Elizabeth I*, Garden City, NY: Doubleday Anchor Books.

Norbrook, David 1984, *Poetry and Politics in the English Renaissance* London: Routledge.

Osgood, Charles 1915, *A Concordance to the Poems of Edmund Spenser*, Publication no. 189, Washington, DC: Carnegie Institute of Washington.

Patterson, Annabel 1984, *Censorship and Interpretation*, Madison: University of Wisconsin Press.

Penniman, Josiah, ed. 1913, *Poetaster and Satiromastix*. Boston: D.C. Heath & Co.

Platz, Norbert 1973, *Jonson's "Ars Poetica": An Interpretation of "Poetaster" in Its Historical Context*, Salzburg Studies in English Literature, 12, University of Salzburg.

Public Record Office, SP 63/94, SP 12/134, SP 12/273. STAC 5 L/34/37 Lincoln v. Dymock. STAC 8 177/05 Harris v. Dixon, Newcomin, Ardley, and Knevett. STAC 8 5/18 Elton v. Davies.

Pulton, Ferdinando 1609, *De pace regis et regni*, London.

Puttenham, George 1936, *The Arte of English Poesie*, Gladys Doidge Willcock and Alice Walker (eds.) Cambridge University Press.

Rambuss, Richard 1993, *Spenser's Secret Career*, Cambridge University Press.

Roche, Thomas 1964, *The Kindly Flame*, Princeton University Press.

Royal Commission of Historical Manuscripts 1872, vol. III, London.

Samaha, Joel 1975, "Gleanings from Local Criminal Court Records: Sedition Amongst the 'Inarticulate' in Elizabethan Essex," *Journal of Social History* 8: 61–79.

Sexton, Joyce 1978, *The Slandered Woman in Shakespeare*, English Literary Studies Monograph no. 12, Victoria, BC: University of Victoria.

Shakespeare, William 1961, *Richard II*, Peter Ure (ed.) London: Methuen.

1965, *Measure for Measure*, J. W. Lever (ed.) London: Methuen.

1969, *Measure for Measure*, J. M. Nosworthy (ed.) London: Penguin.
1982, *Hamlet*, Harold Jenkins (ed.) London: Methuen.
1982, *Troilus and Cressida*, Kenneth Palmer (ed.) London: Methuen.
Sharpe, J. A. 1980, *Defamation and Sexual Slander in Early Modern England*, Borthwick Papers no. 58, University of York, Borthwick Institute of Historical Research.
Sisson, C. J. 1936, *Lost Plays of Shakespeare's Age*, Cambridge University Press.
Smith, A. Hassel 1974, *County and Court: Government and Politics in Norfolk, 1558–1603*, Oxford: Clarendon.
Spencer, Christopher 1965, "Lucio and the Friar's Hood," *English Language Notes* 3: 17–21.
Spenser, Edmund 1934, *A View of the Present State of Ireland*, W. L. Renwick (ed.) London: Eric Partridge, Ltd.
1977, *The Faerie Queene*, A. C. Hamilton (ed.) London: Longman.
Statutes of the Realm 1587, London.
Stephen, H. L. 1899, *State Trials Political and Social*, vol. II, London: Duckworth and Co.
Stone, Lawrence 1967, *The Crisis of the Aristocracy*, abridged version, Oxford University Press.
Strong, Roy 1963, *Portraits of Queen Elizabeth I*, Oxford: Clarendon.
Talbert, Ernest William 1945, "The Purpose and Technique of Jonson's *Poetaster*," *Studies in Philology* 42: 225–52.
Waith, Eugene 1951, "The Poet's Morals in Jonson's *Poetaster*," *Modern Language Quarterly* 12: 13–19.

Index

Cambridge Studies in Renaissance Literature and Culture

General editor
STEPHEN ORGEL
Jackson Eli Reynolds Professor of Humanities, Stanford University

1. Douglas Bruster, University of Chicago *Drama and the market in the age of Shakespeare*
2. Virginia Cox, University College London *The Renaissance dialogue: literary dialogue in its social and political contexts, Castiglione to Galileo*
3. Richard Rambuss, Emory University *Spencer's secret career*
4. John Gillies, La Trobe University *Shakespeare and the geography of difference*
5. Laura Levine, Wellesley College *Men in women's clothing: anti-theatricality and effeminization, 1579–1642*
6. Linda Gregerson, University of Michigan *The reformation of the subject: Spenser, Milton, and the English Protestant epic*
7. Mary C. Fuller, Massachusetts Institute of Technology *Voyages in print: English travel in America, 1576–1624*
8. edited by Margreta de Grazia, Maureen Quilligan, Peter Stallybrass, University of Pennsylvania *Subject and object in Renaissance culture*
9. T. G. Bishop, Case Western Reserve University *Shakespeare and the theatre of wonder*
10. Mark Breitenberg *Anxious masculinity in early modern England*
11. Frank Whigham, University of Texas at Austin *Seizures of the will in early modern English drama*
12. Kevin Pask *The emergence of the English author: scripting the life of the poet in early modern England*
13. Claire McEachern, University of California, Los Angeles *The poetics of English nationhood, 1590–1612*
14. Jeffrey Masten, Harvard University *Textual intercourse: collaboration, authorship, and sexualities in Renaissance drama*
15. Timothy J. Reiss, New York University *Knowledge, discovery and imagination in early modern Europe: the rise of aesthetic rationalism*

16. edited by Elizabeth Fowler, Yale University, and Roland Greene, University of Oregon *The project of prose in early modern Europe and the New World*

17. Alexandra Halasz, Dartmouth College *The marketplace of print: pamphlets and the public sphere in early modern England*

18. Seth Lerer, Stanford University *Courtly letters in the age of Henry VIII: literary culture and the arts of deceit*

19. M. Lindsay Kaplan, Georgetown University *The culture of slander in early modern England*

Lightning Source UK Ltd.
Milton Keynes UK
UKOW05f0630241014

240537UK00001BB/171/P